The Great Canadian
Cottage Colouring Book

Paul Covello & Leor Boshi

Collins

The Great Canadian Cottage Colouring Book
Copyright © 2016 by HarperCollins Publishers Ltd
All rights reserved.

Published by Collins, an imprint of HarperCollins Publishers Ltd

First Edition

HarperCollins books may be purchased for educational, business,
or sales promotional use through our Special Markets Department.

HarperCollins Publishers Ltd
2 Bloor Street East, 20th Floor,
Toronto, Ontario, Canada M4W 1A8

www.harpercollins.ca

Library and Archives Canada Cataloguing in Publication
information is available upon request.

ISBN 978-1-44345-093-5

Printed in China
LEO 10 9 8 7 6 5 4 3 2 1

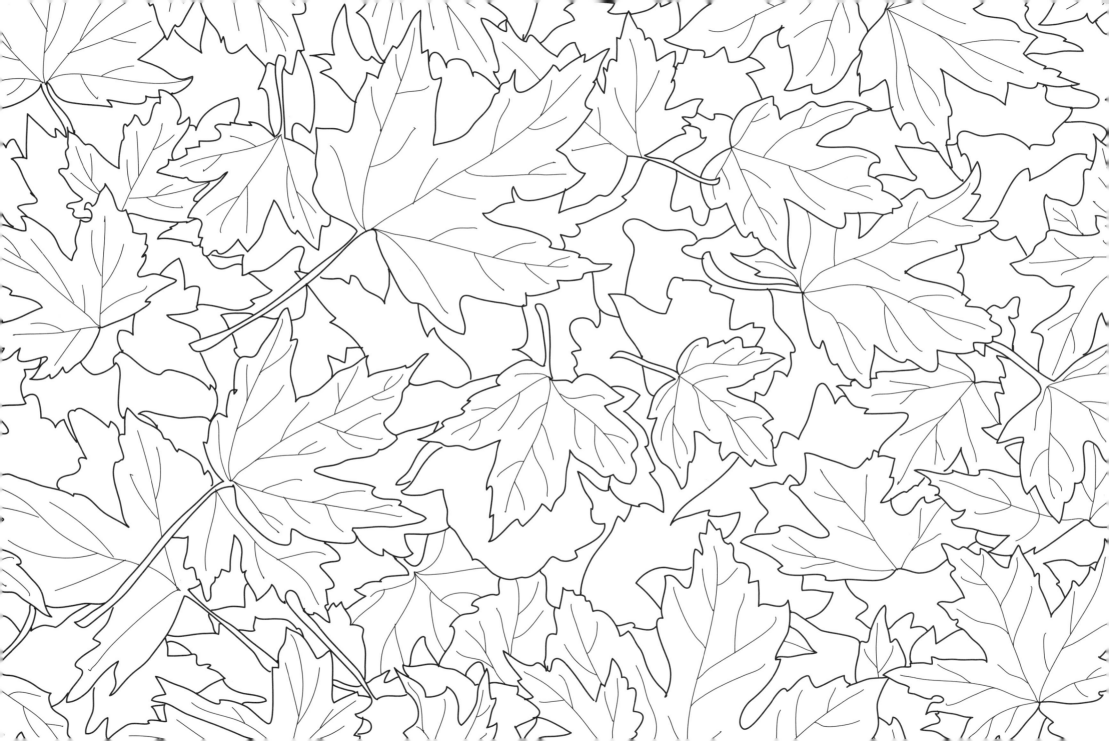

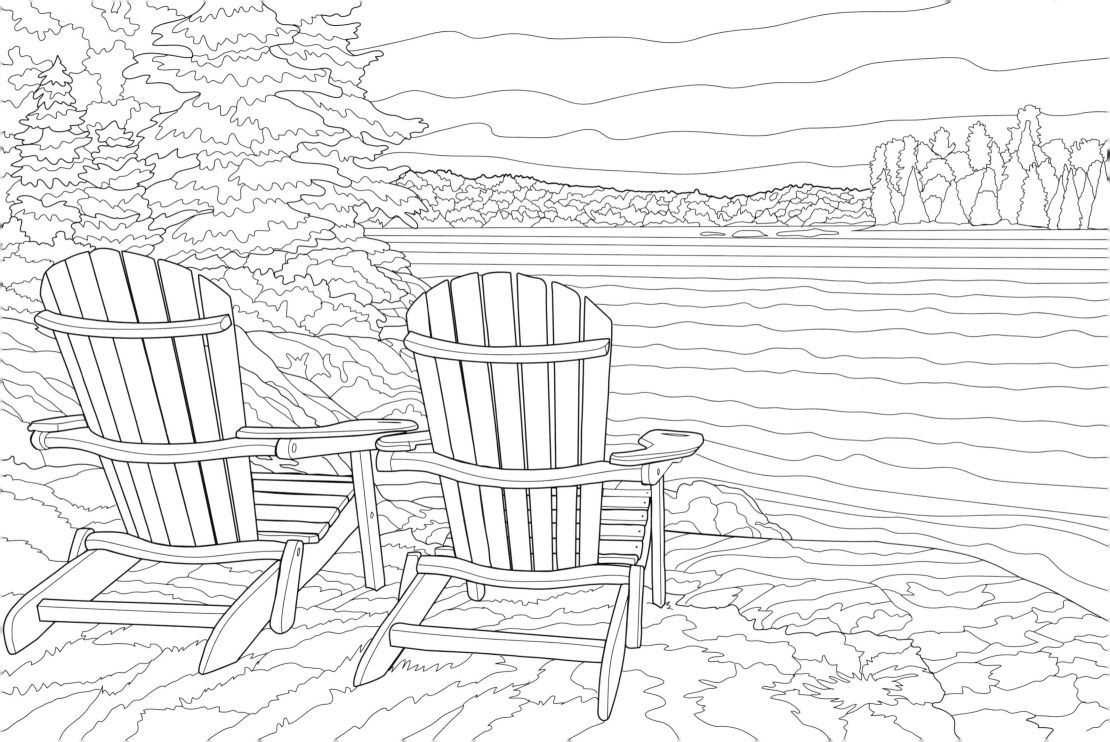

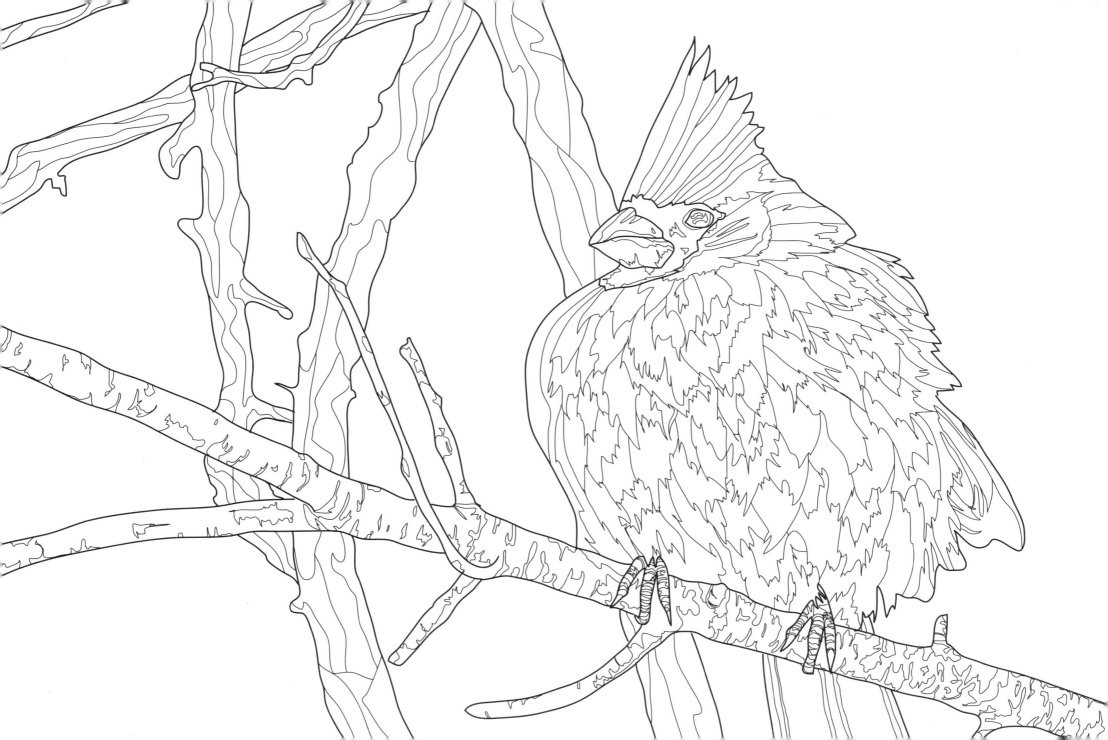

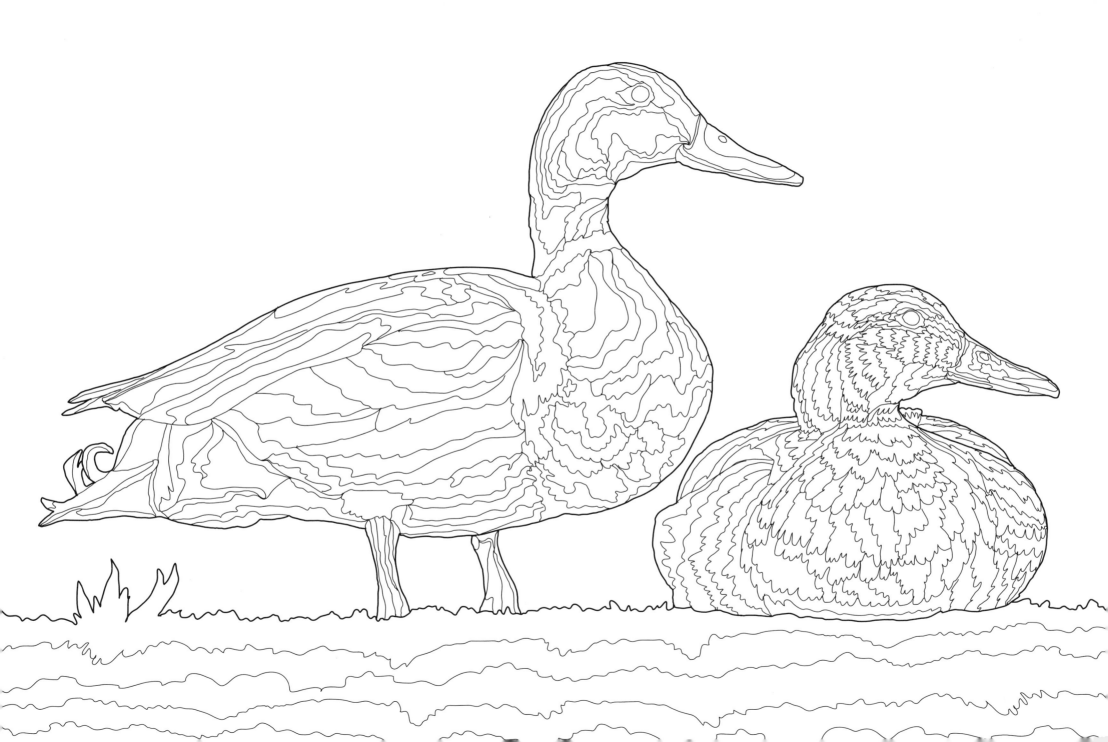

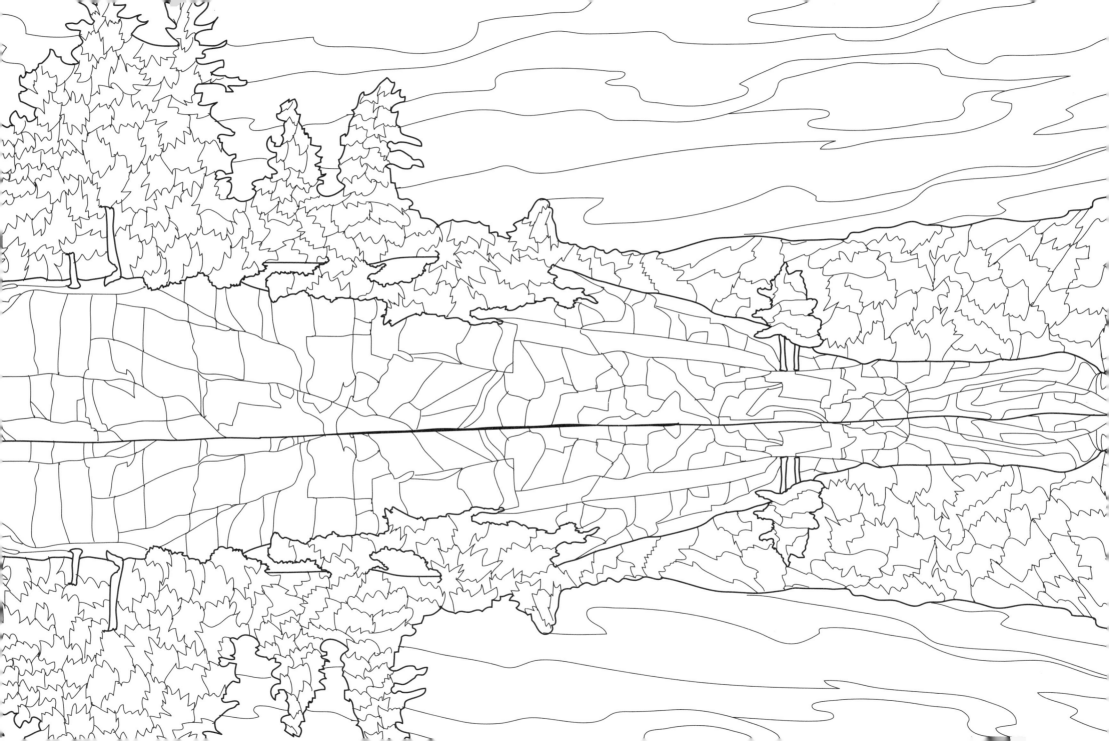

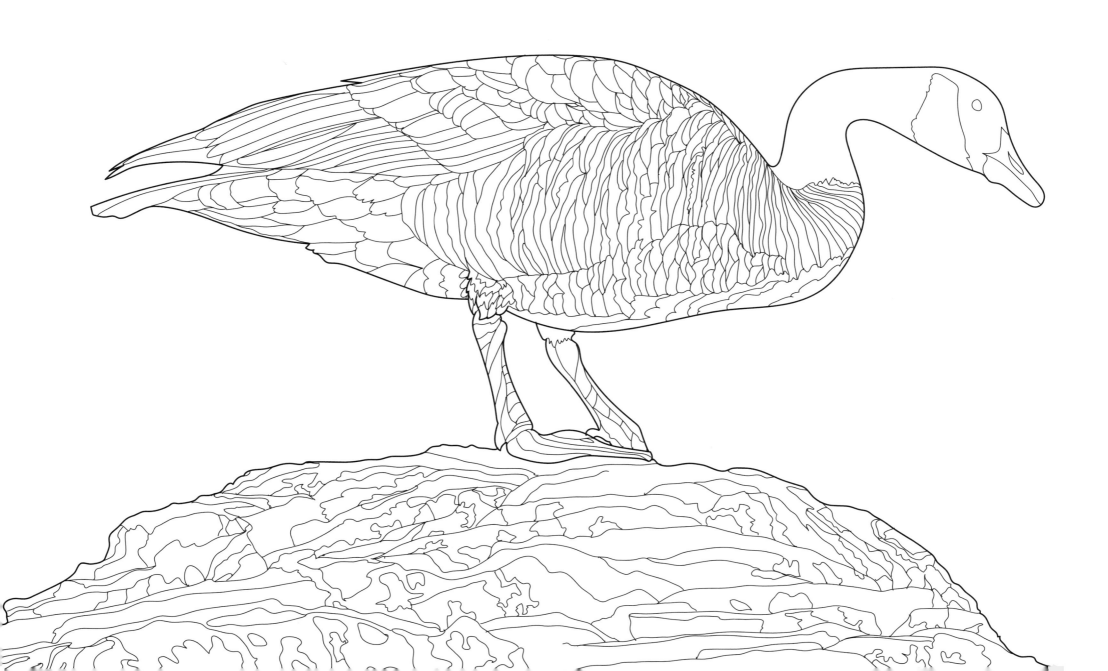

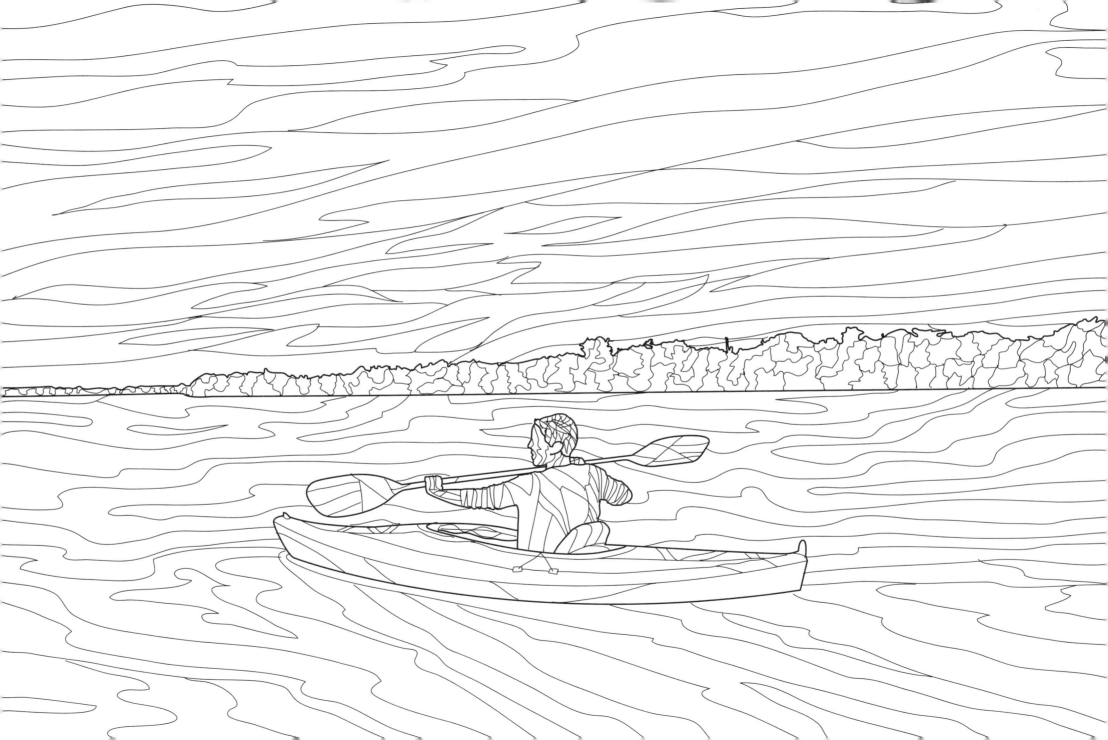

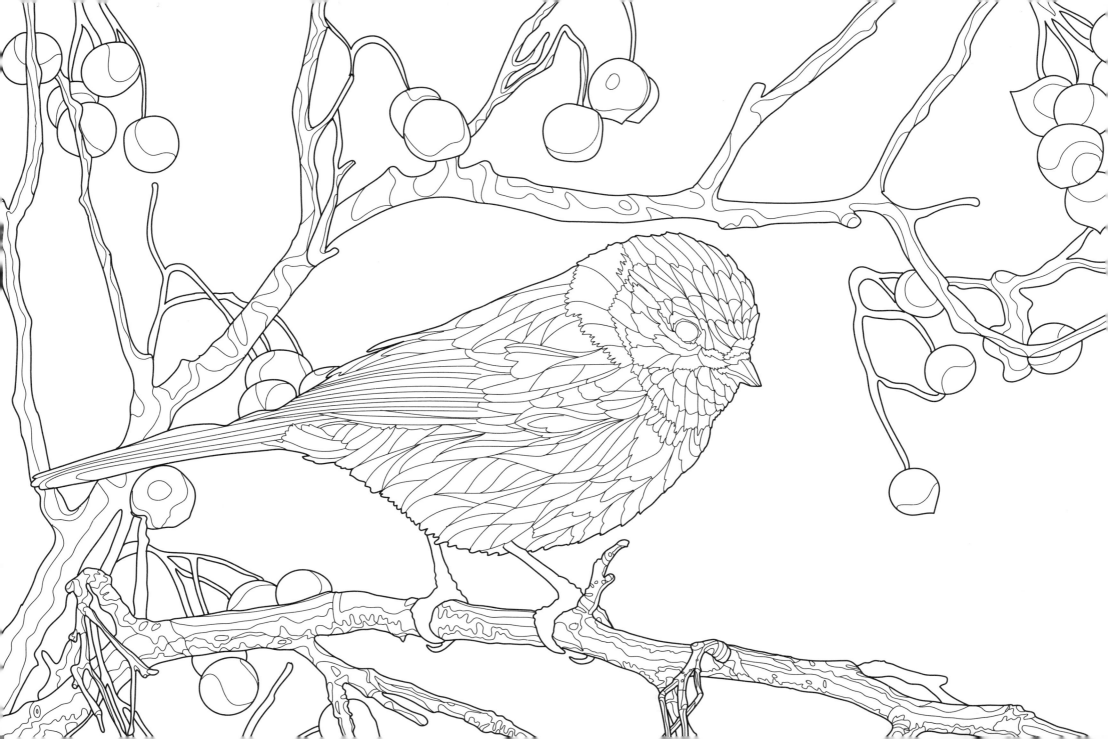

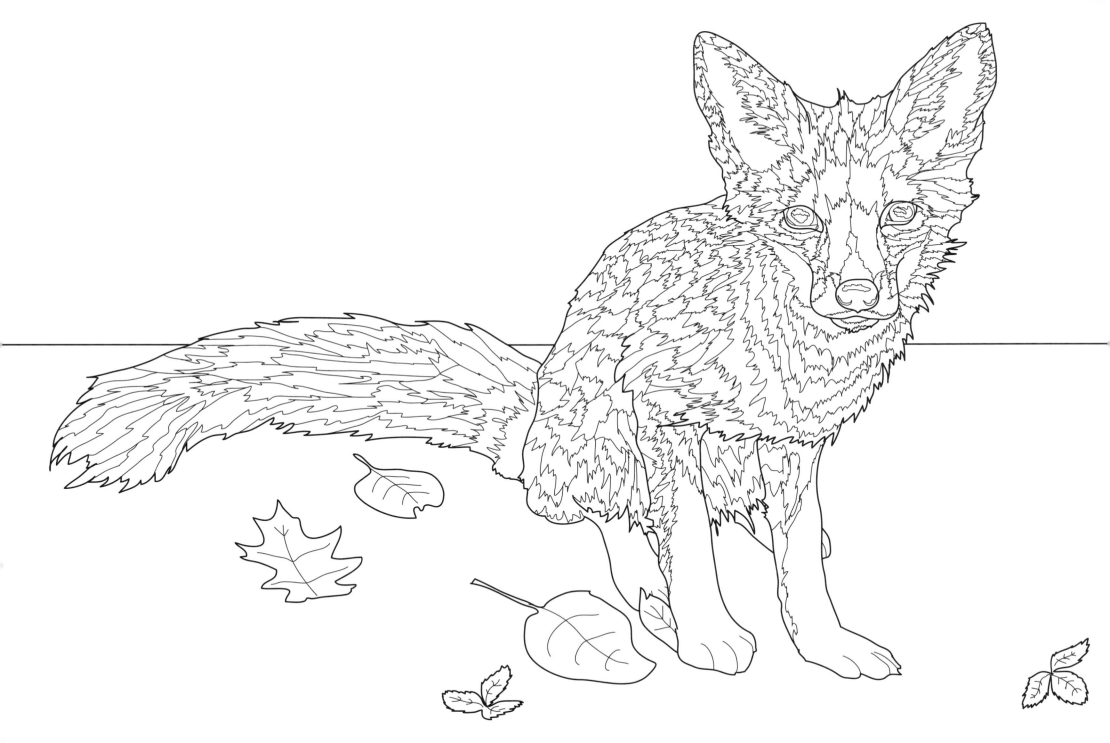

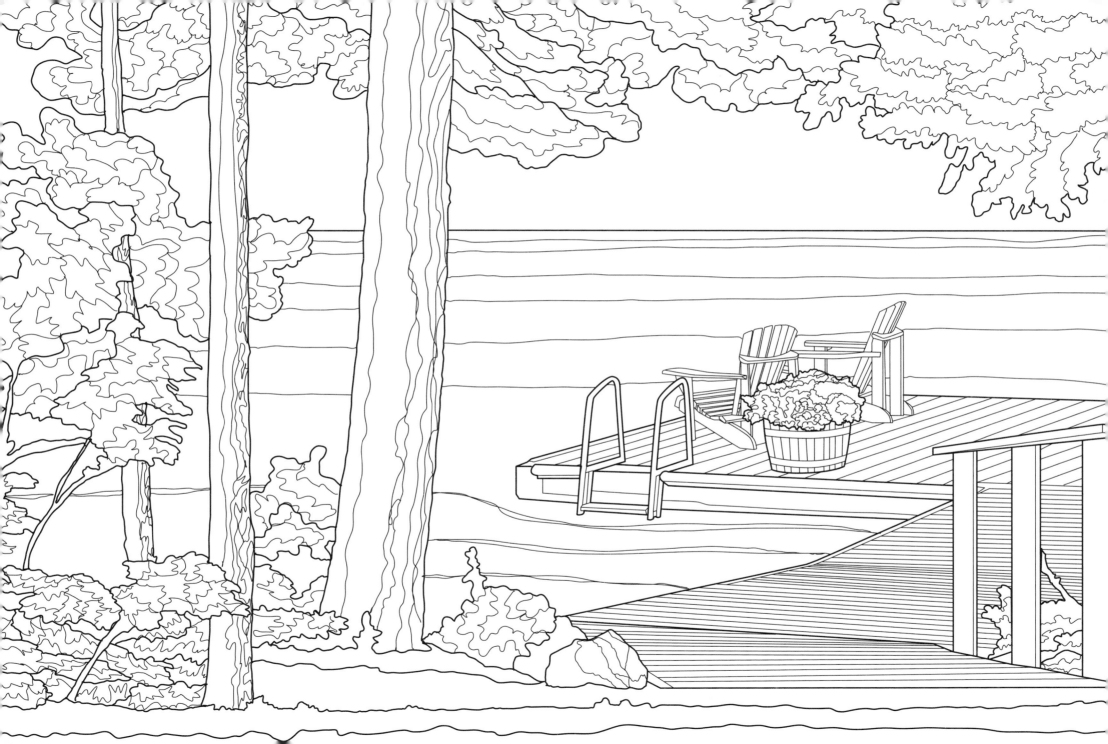

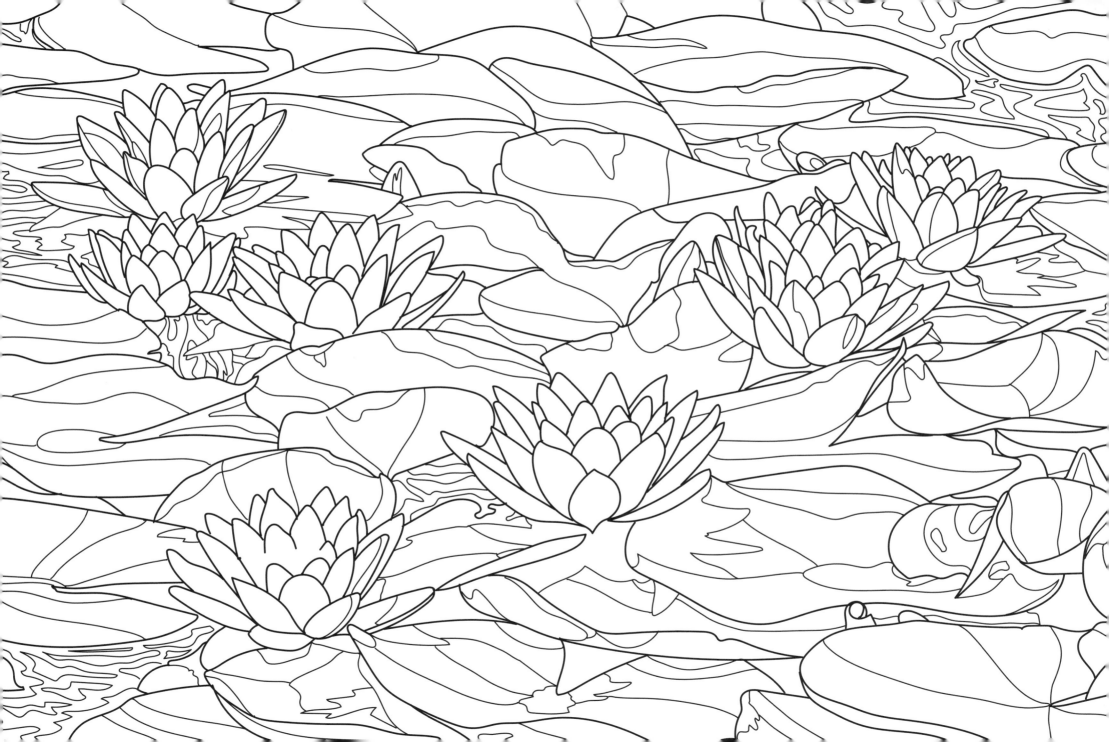

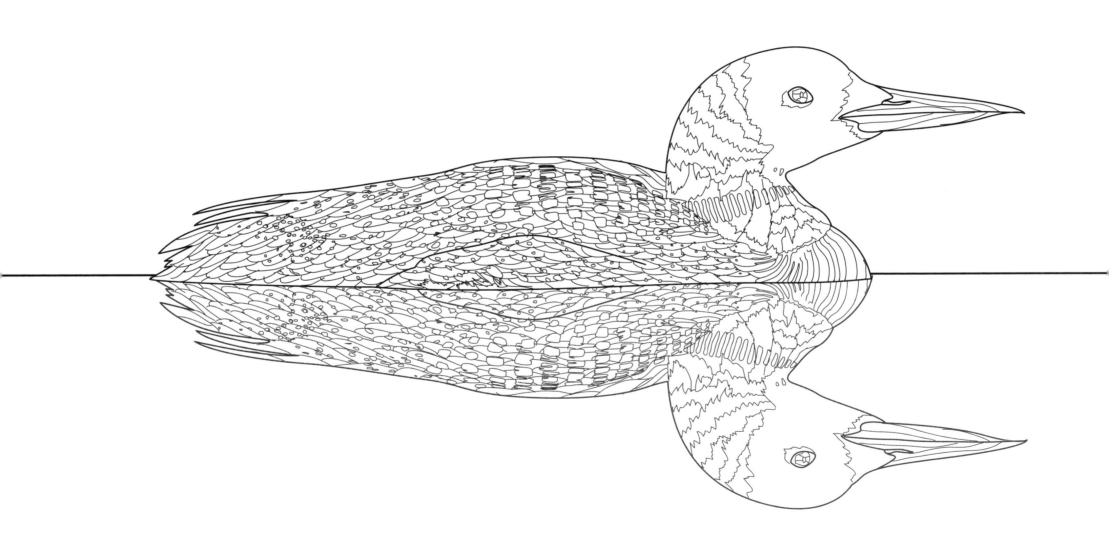

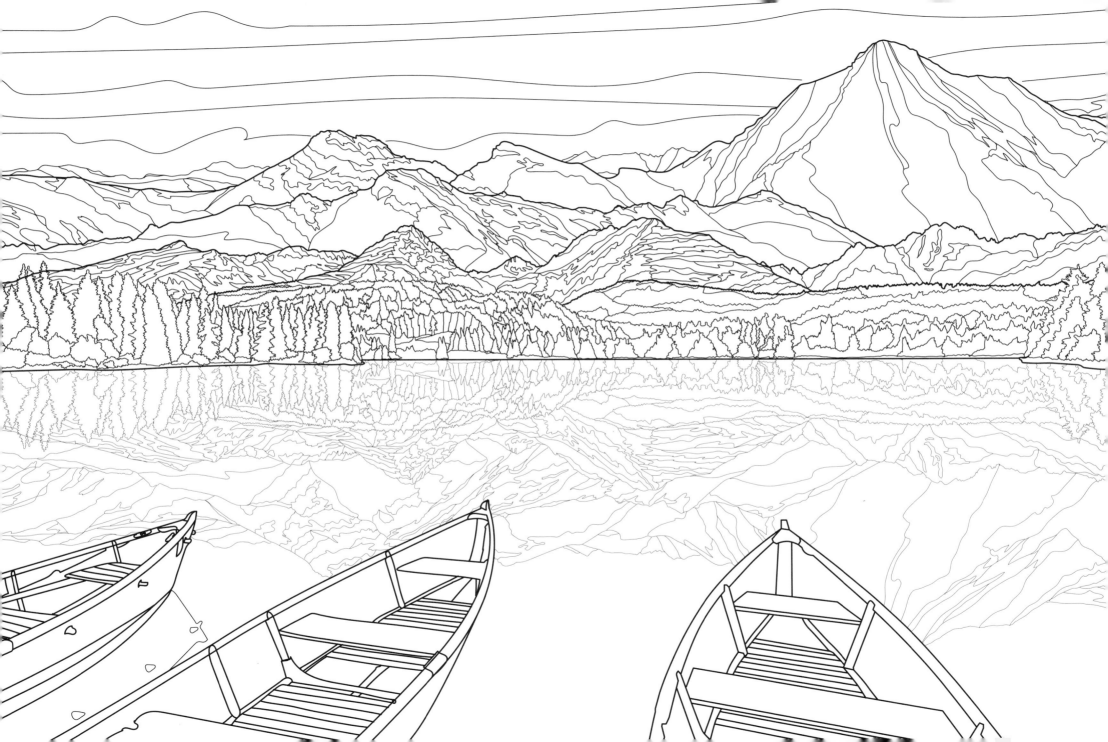

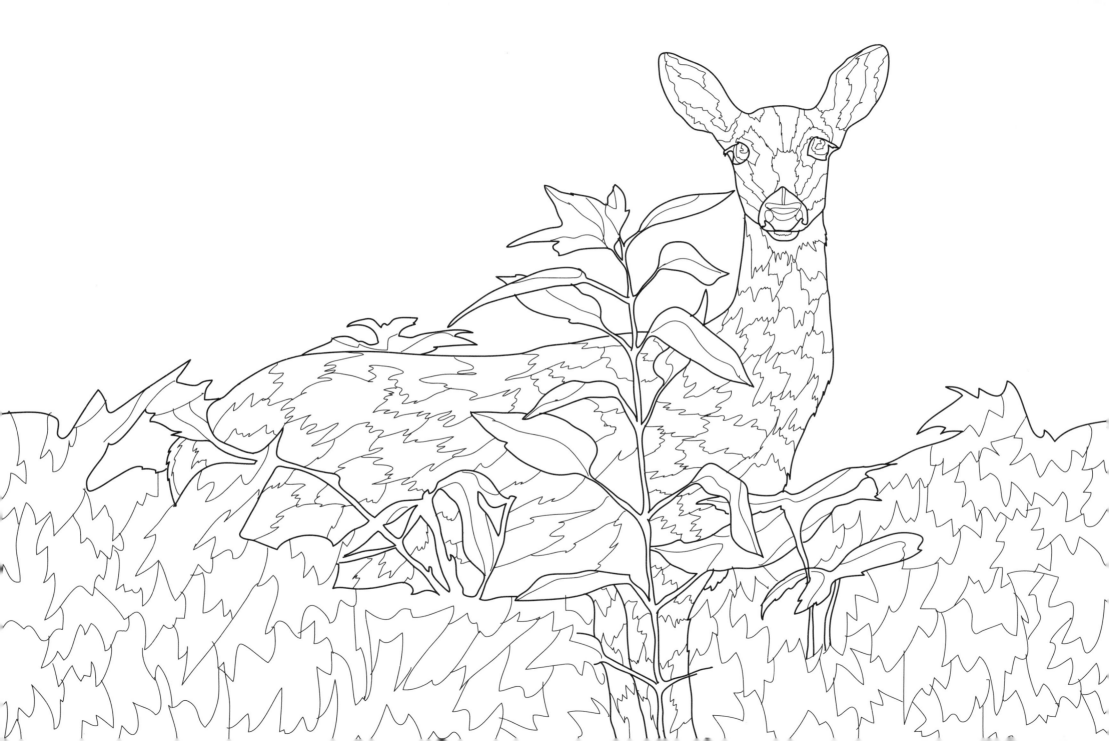

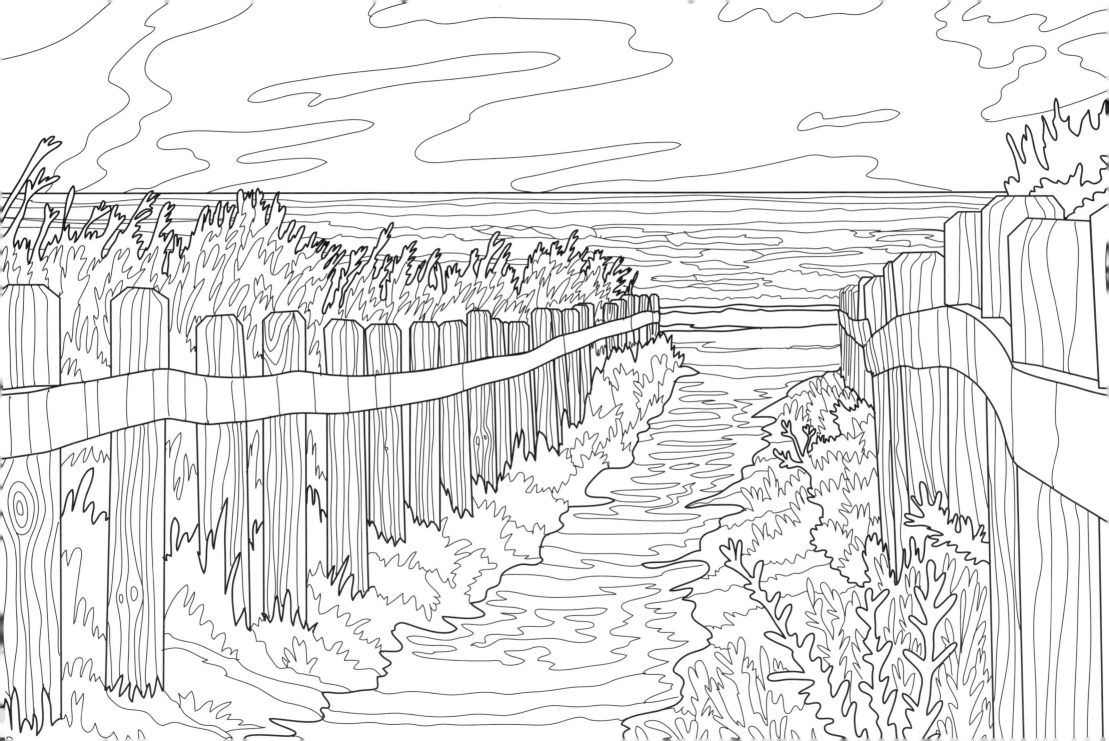

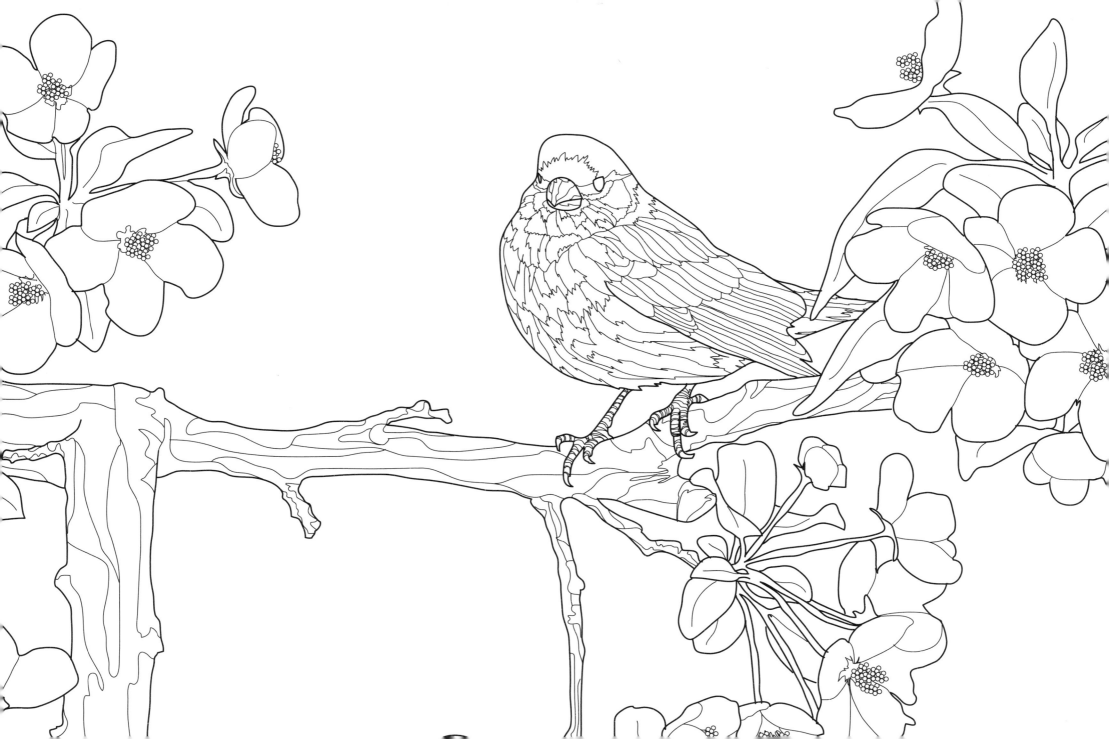

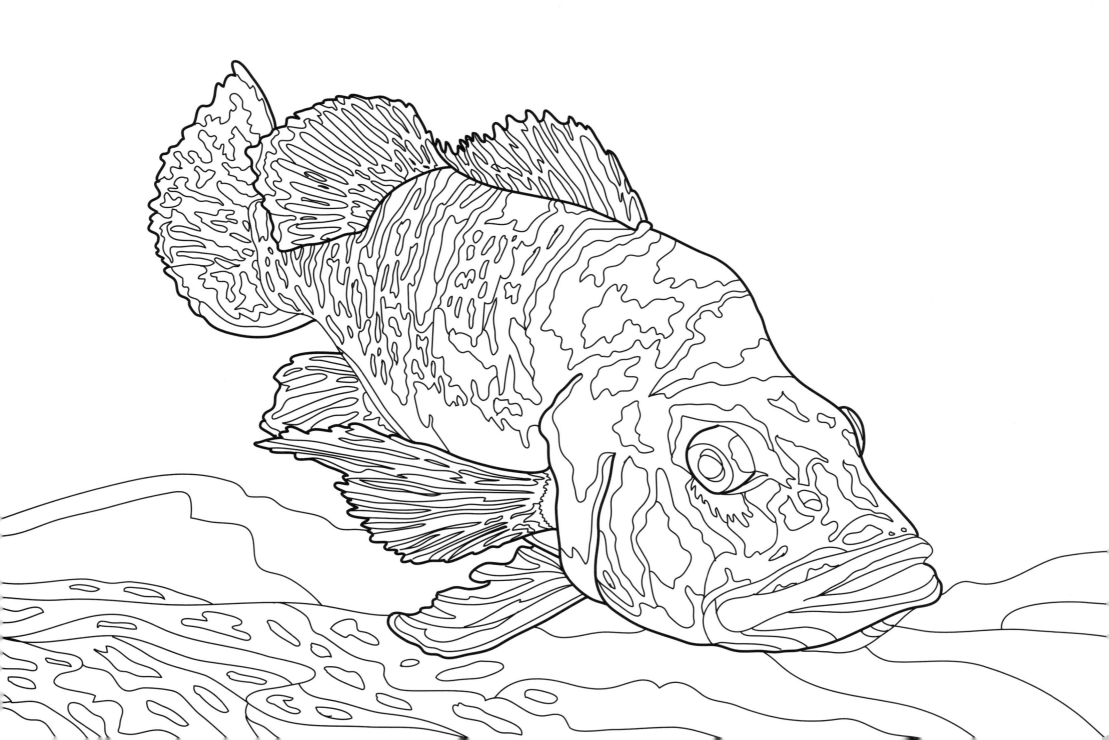

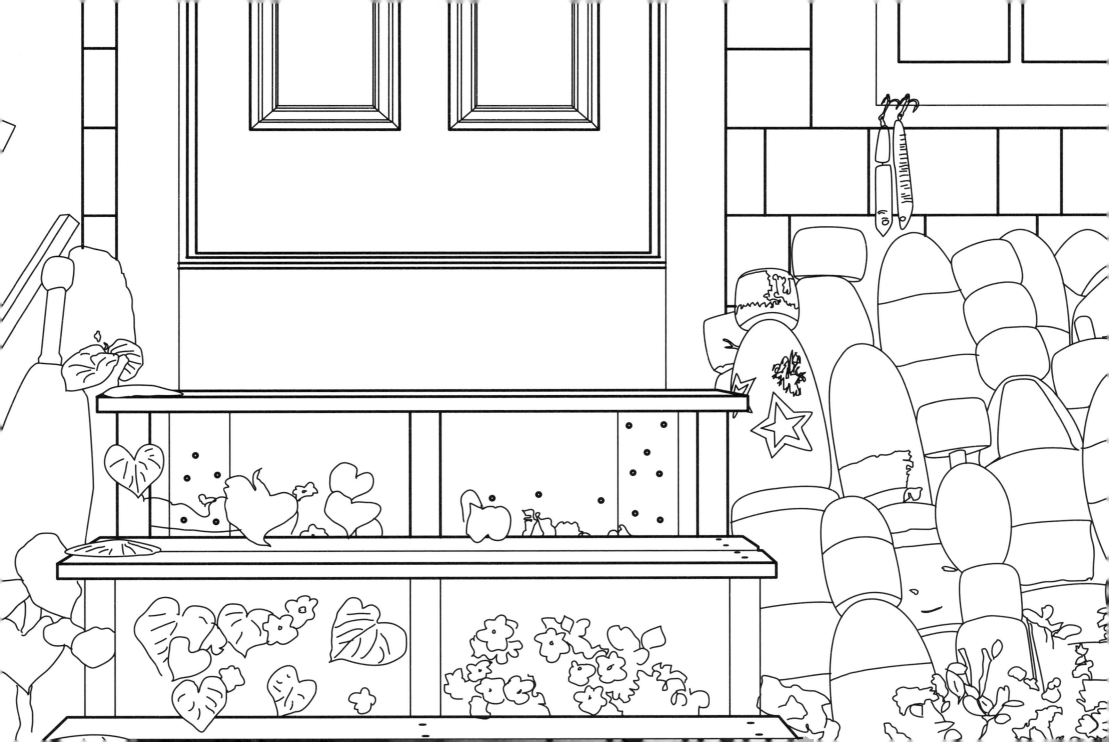

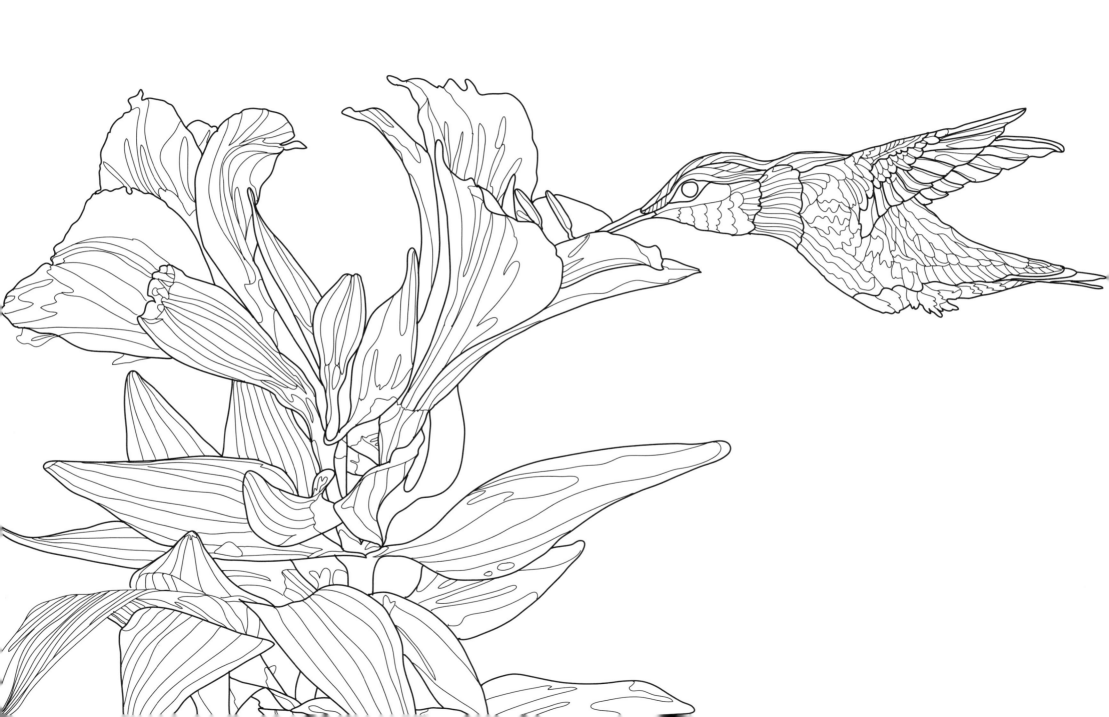

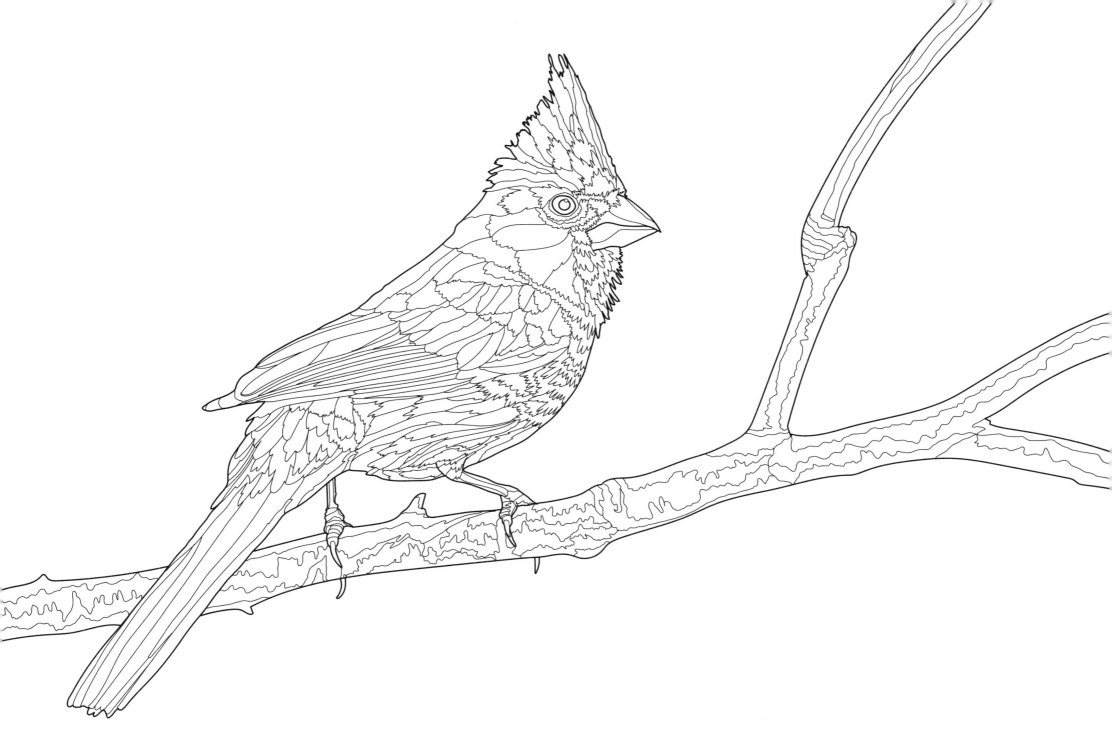

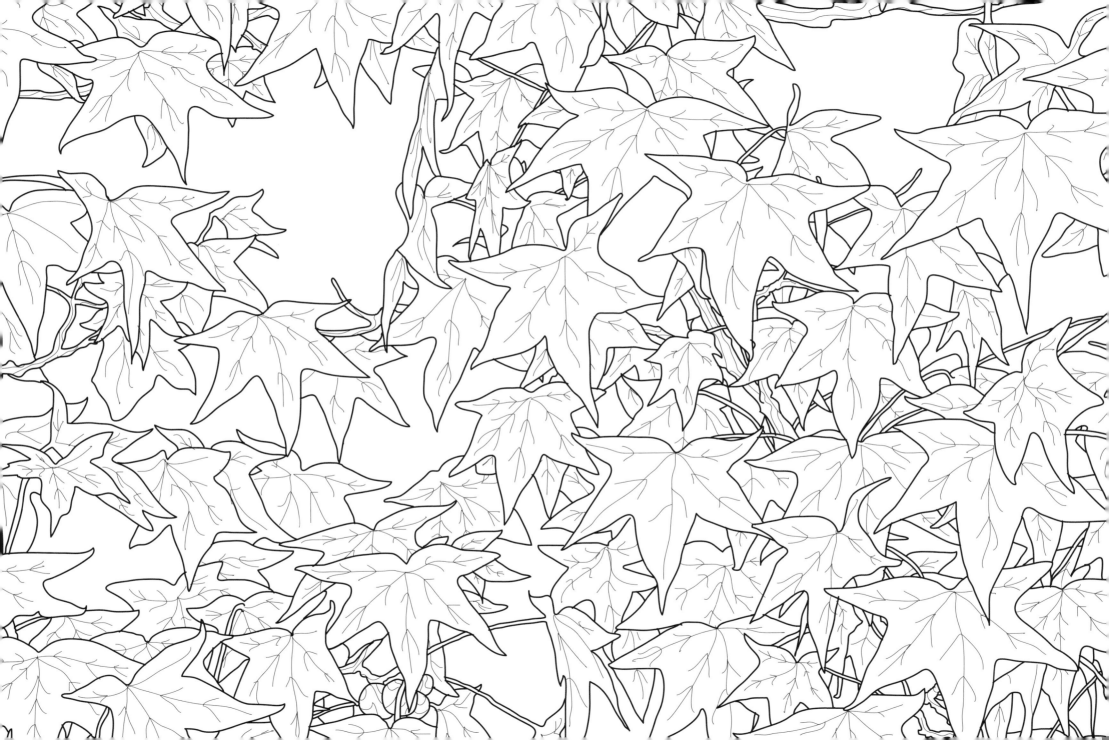

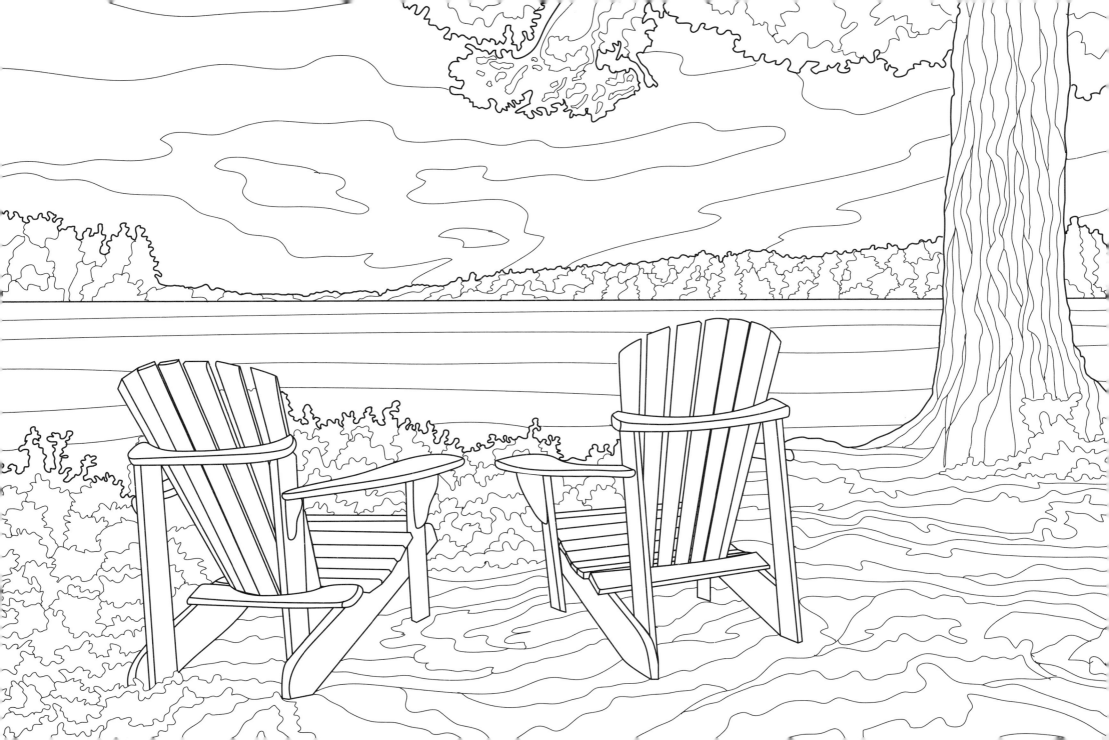

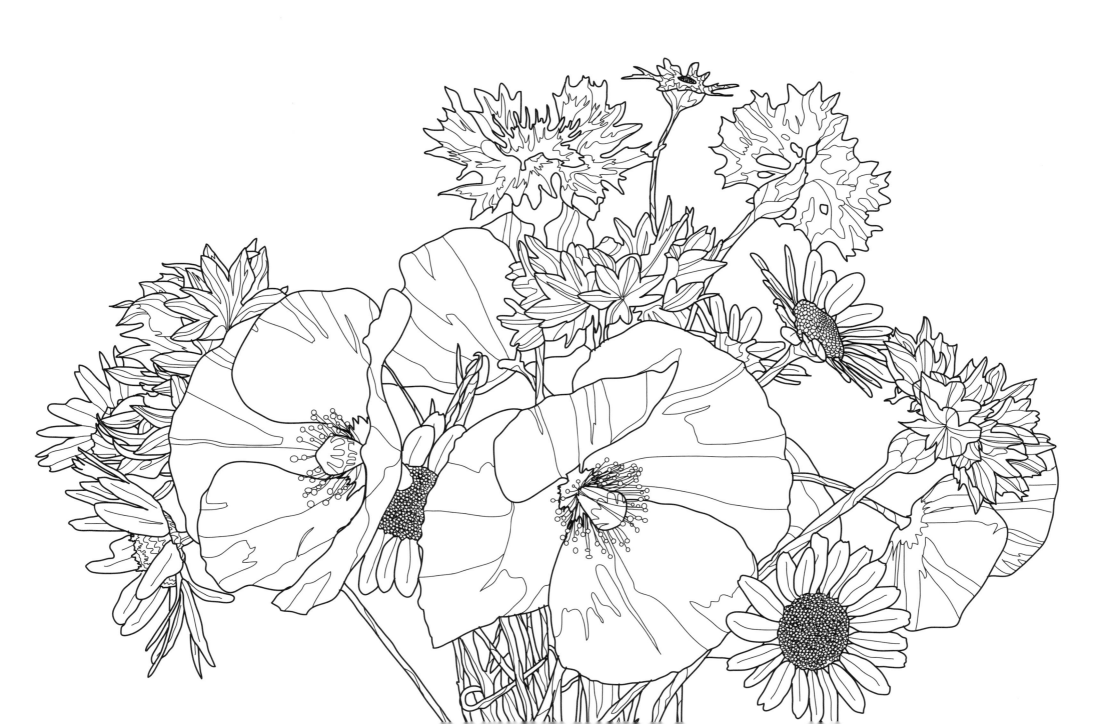

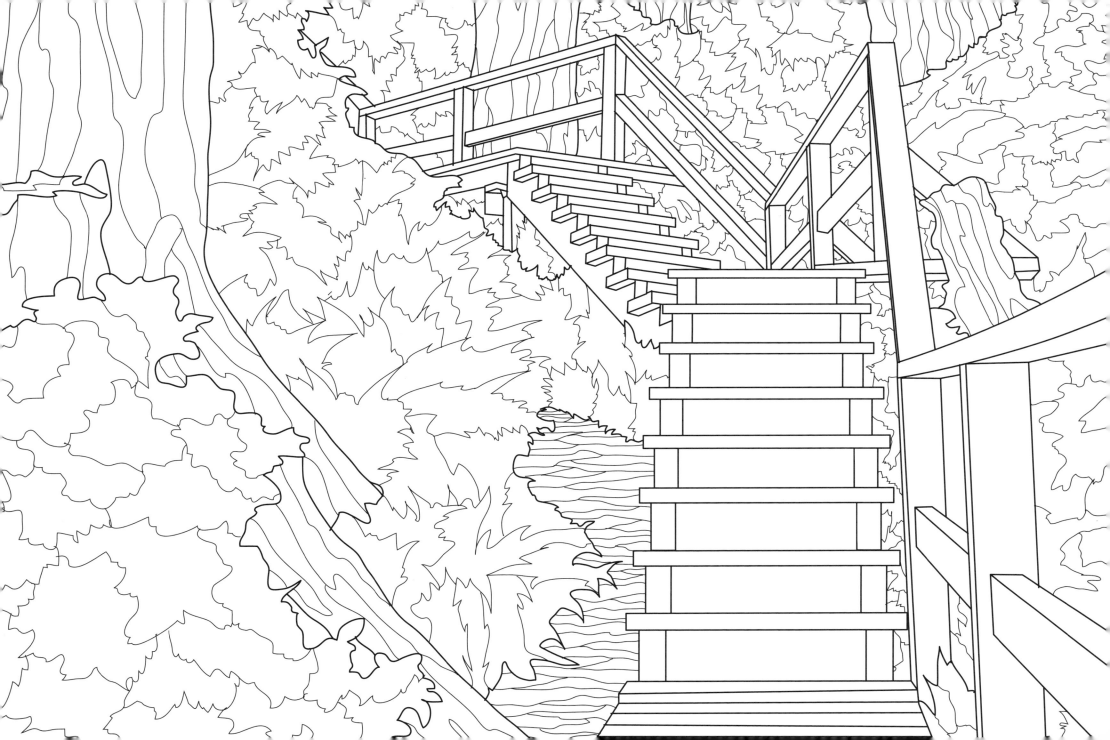

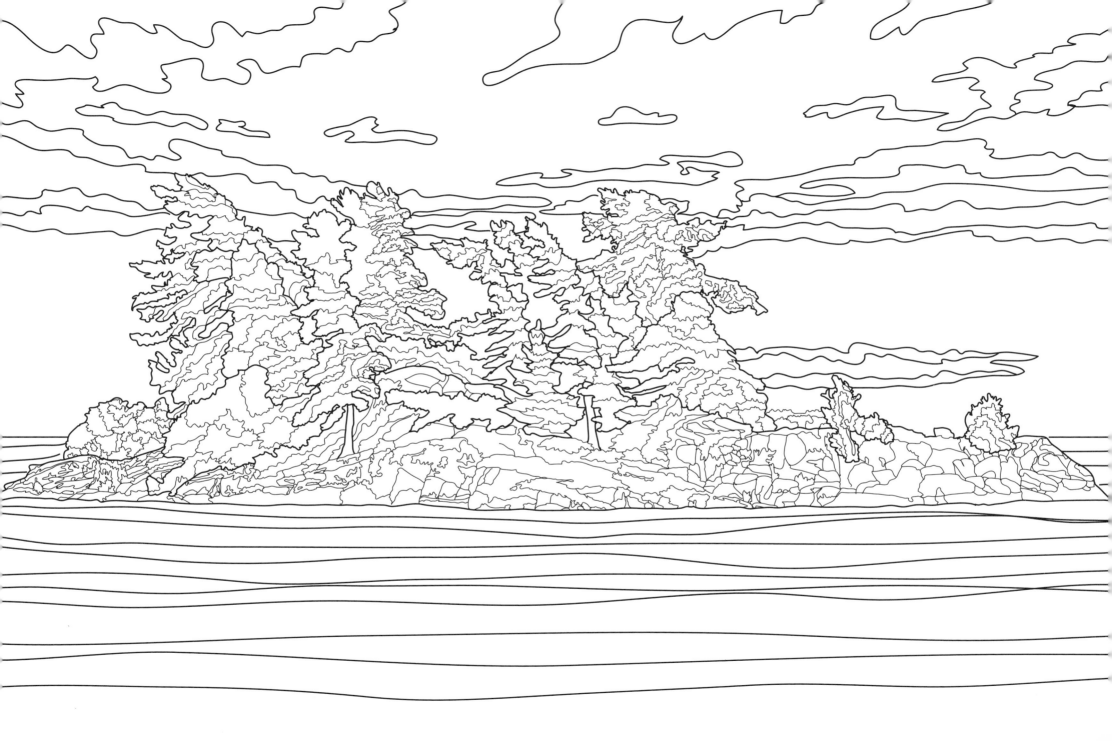

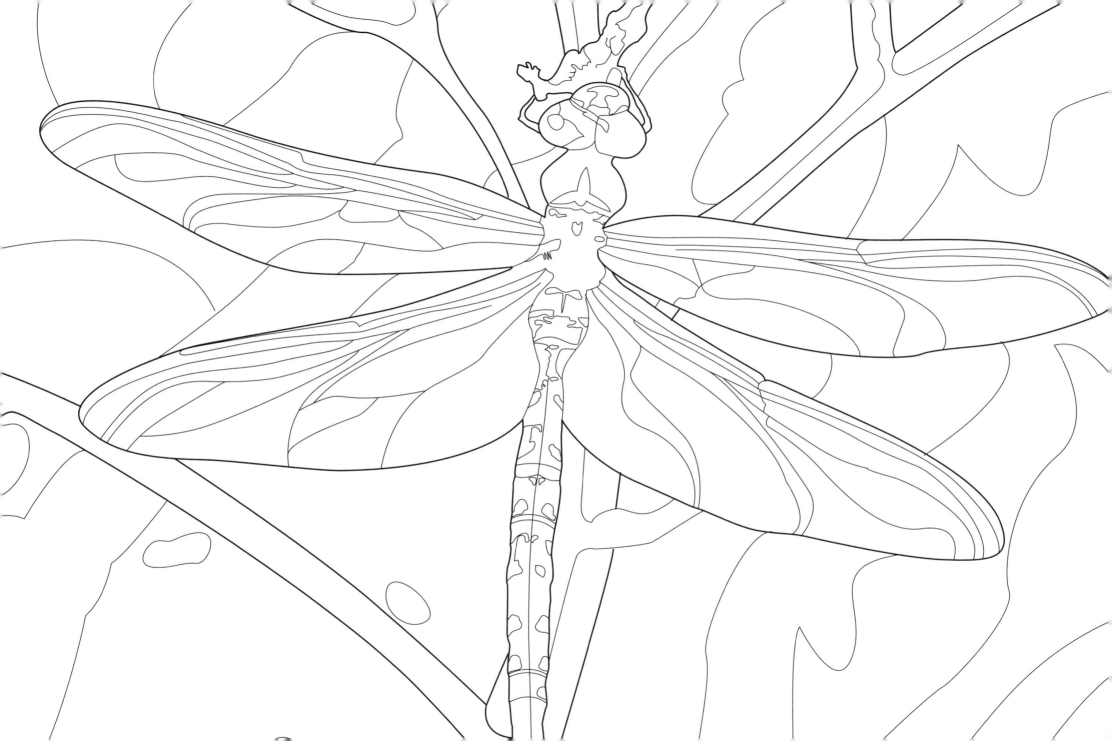

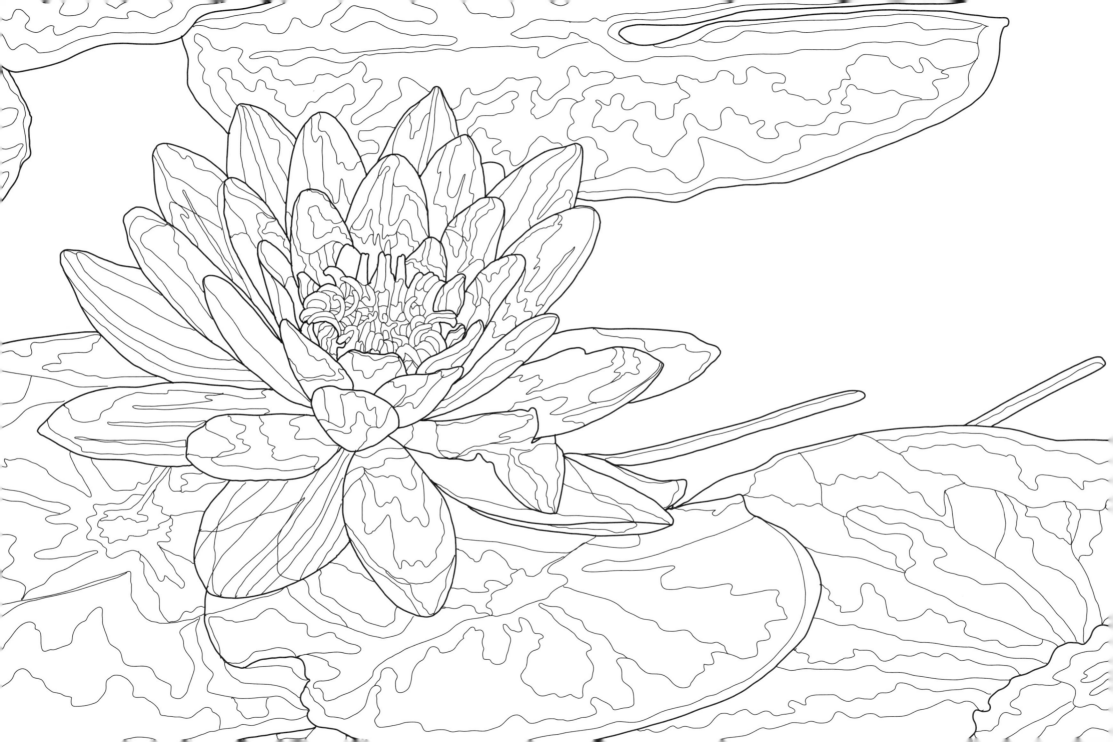

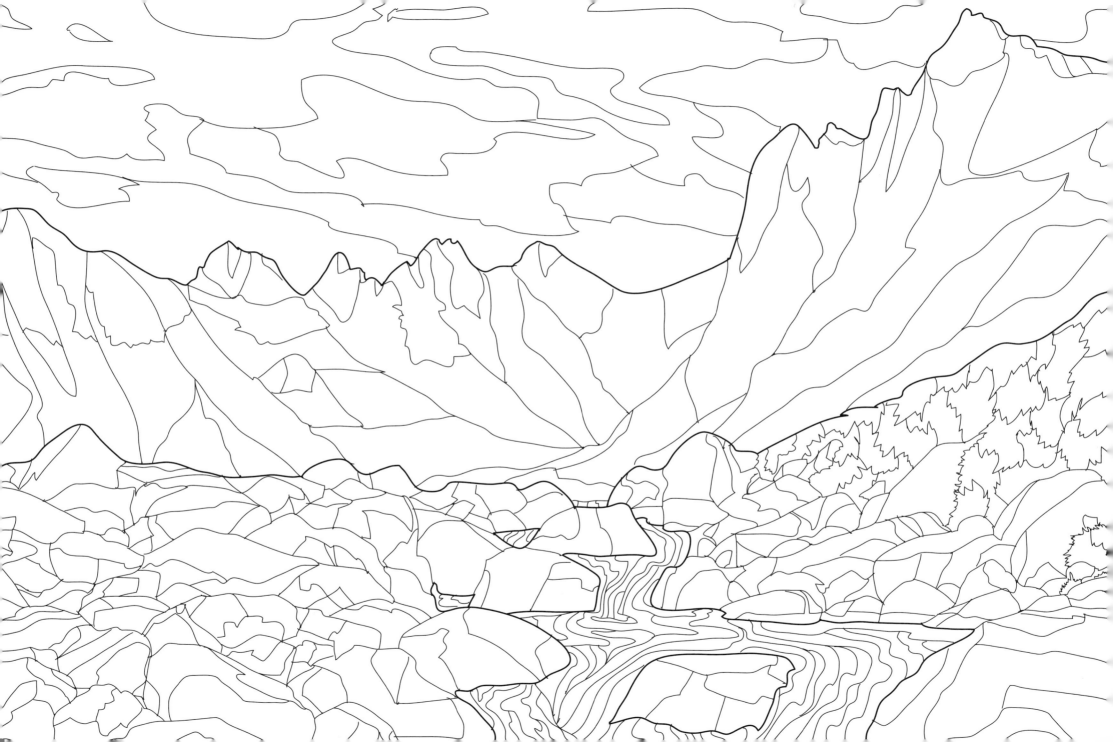

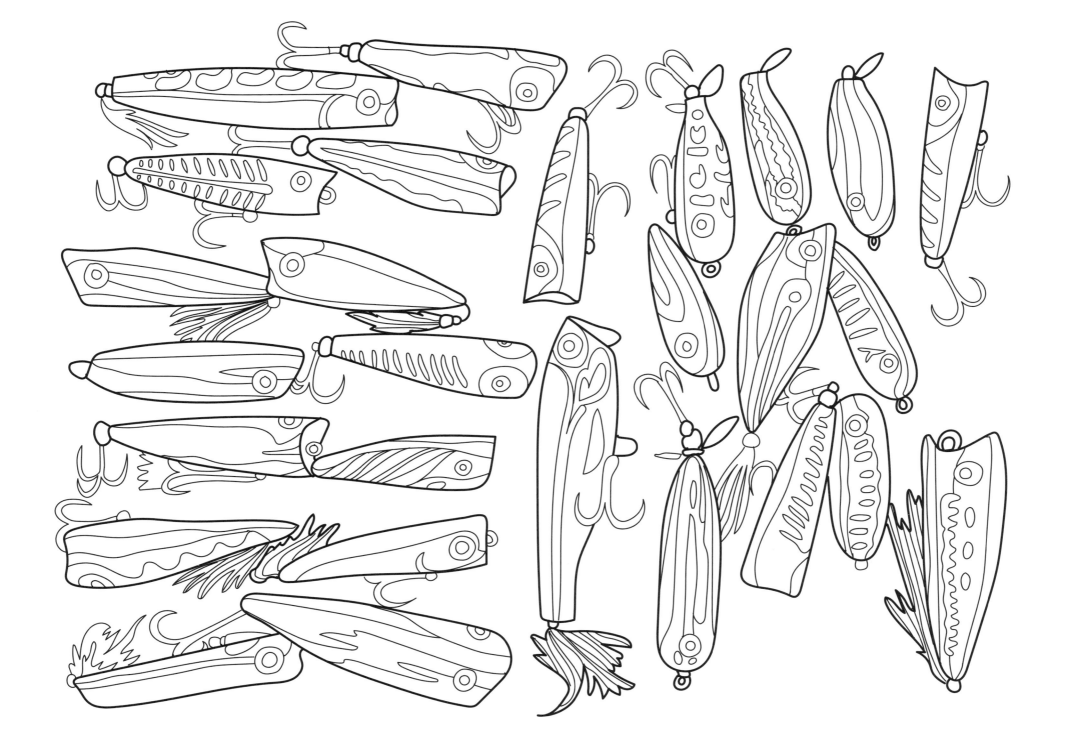

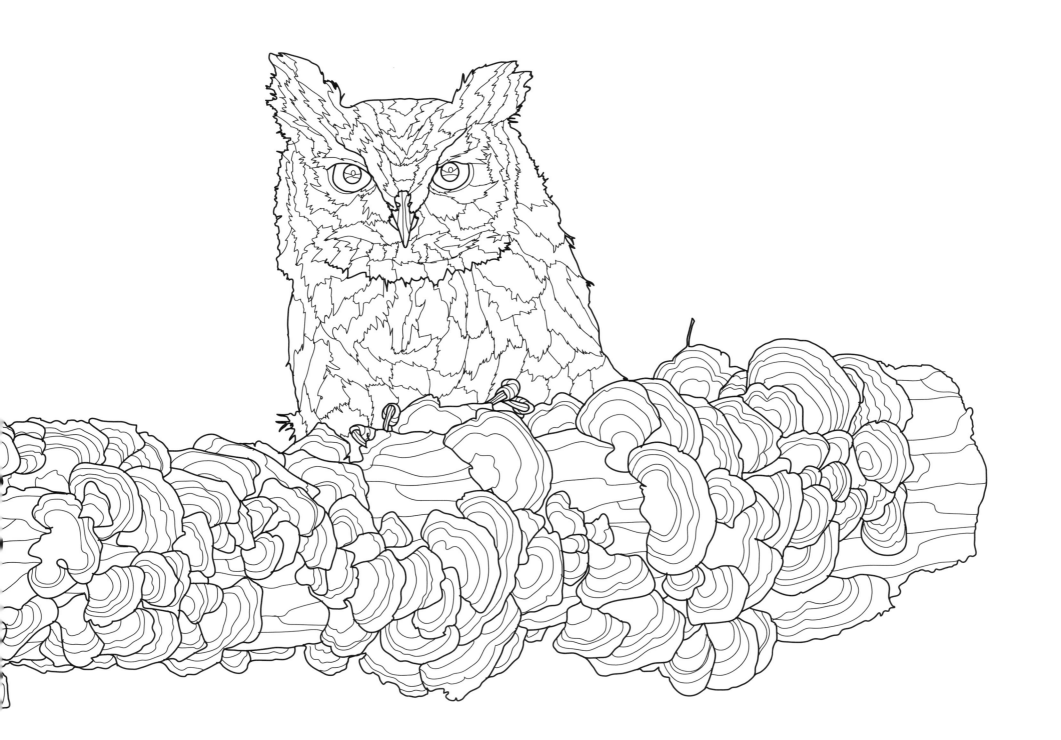

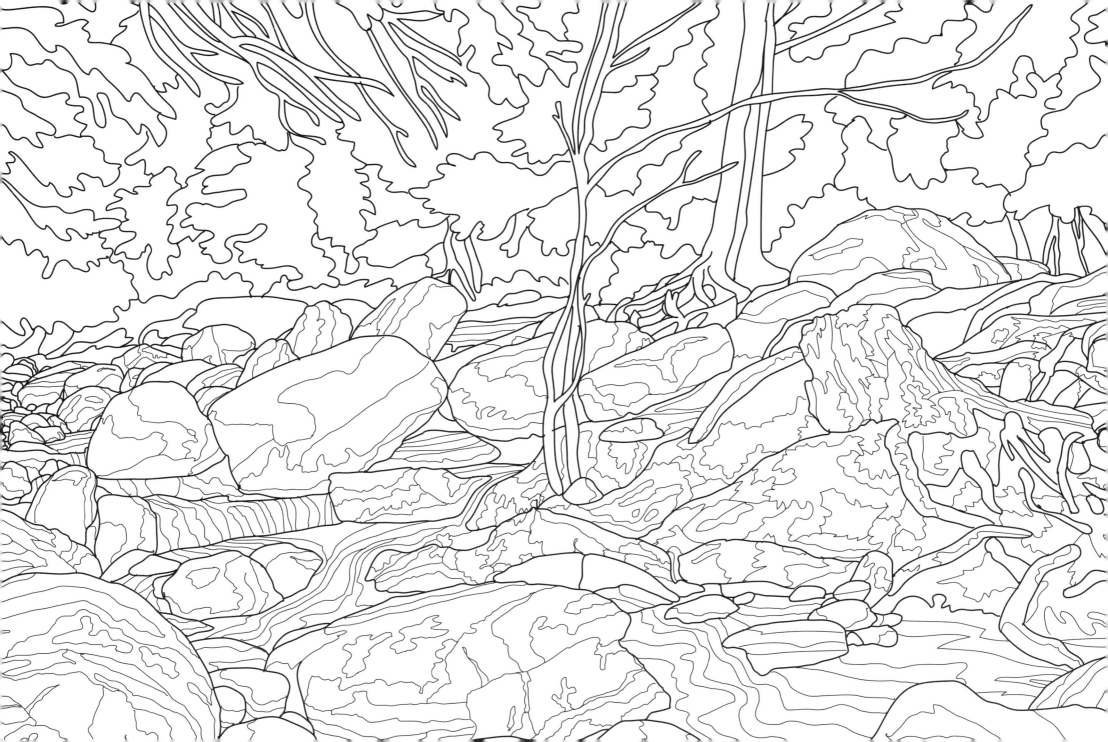

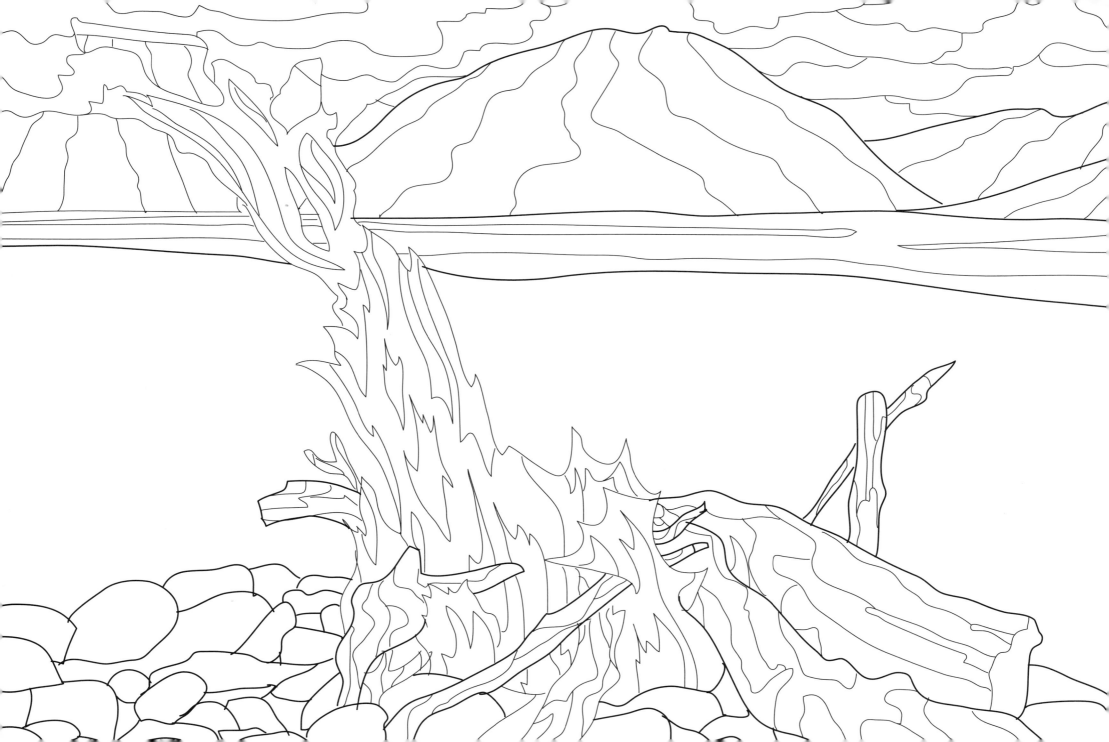

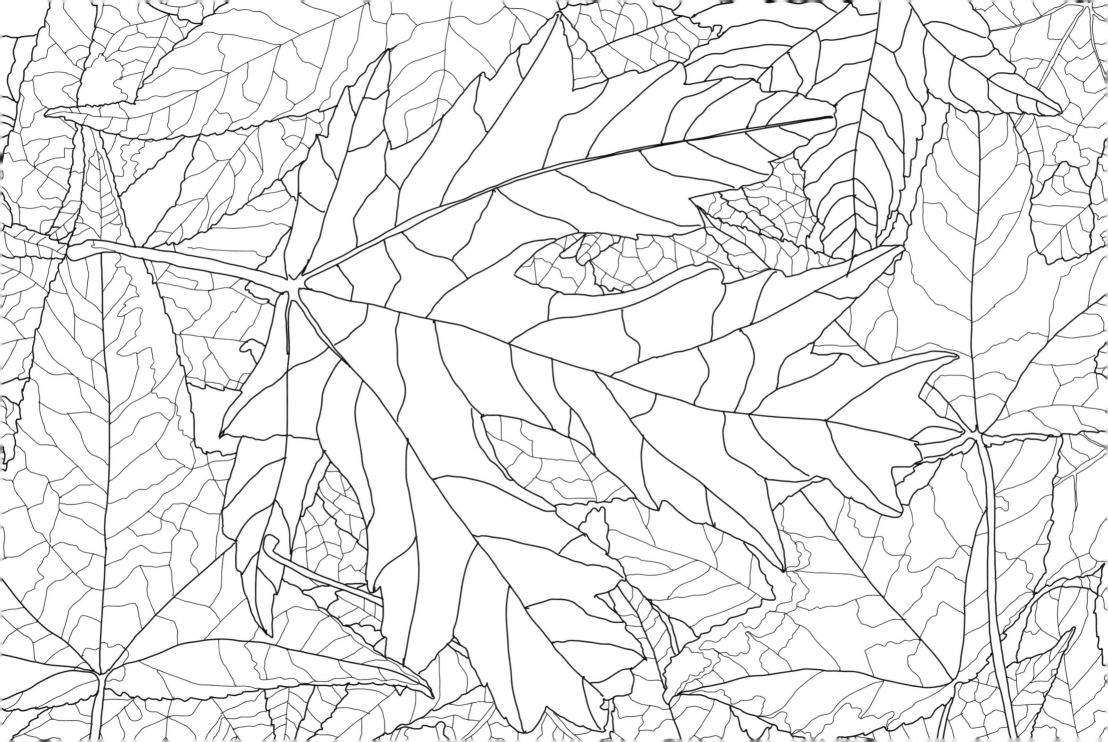

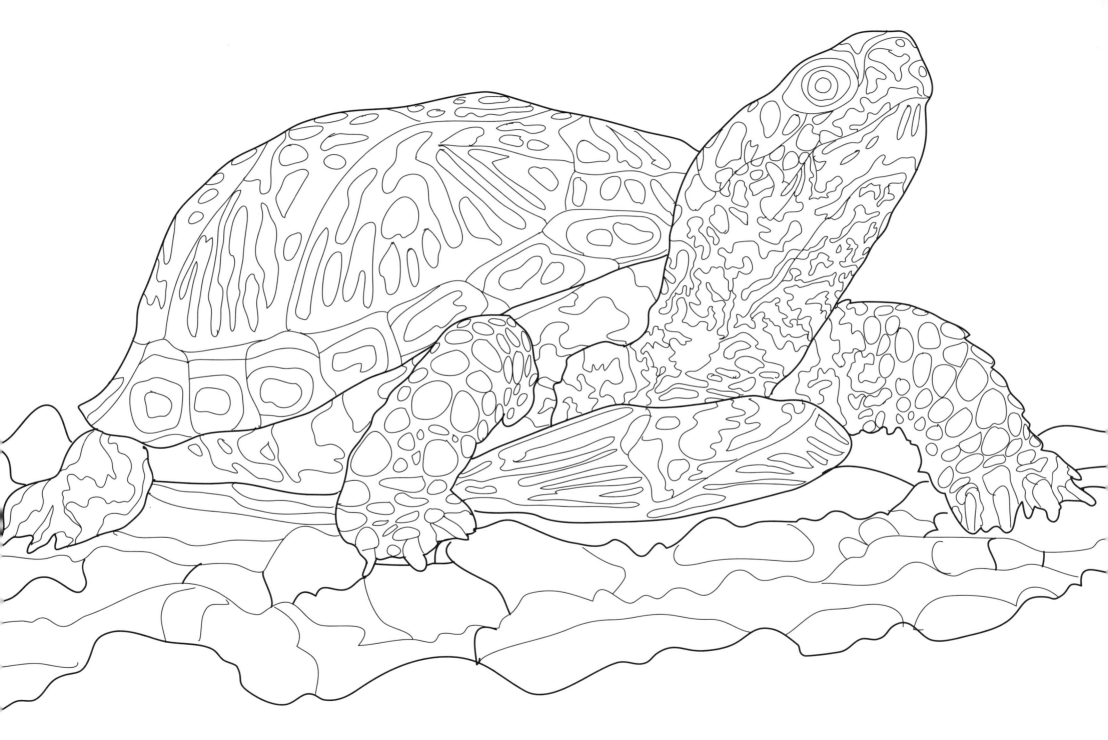

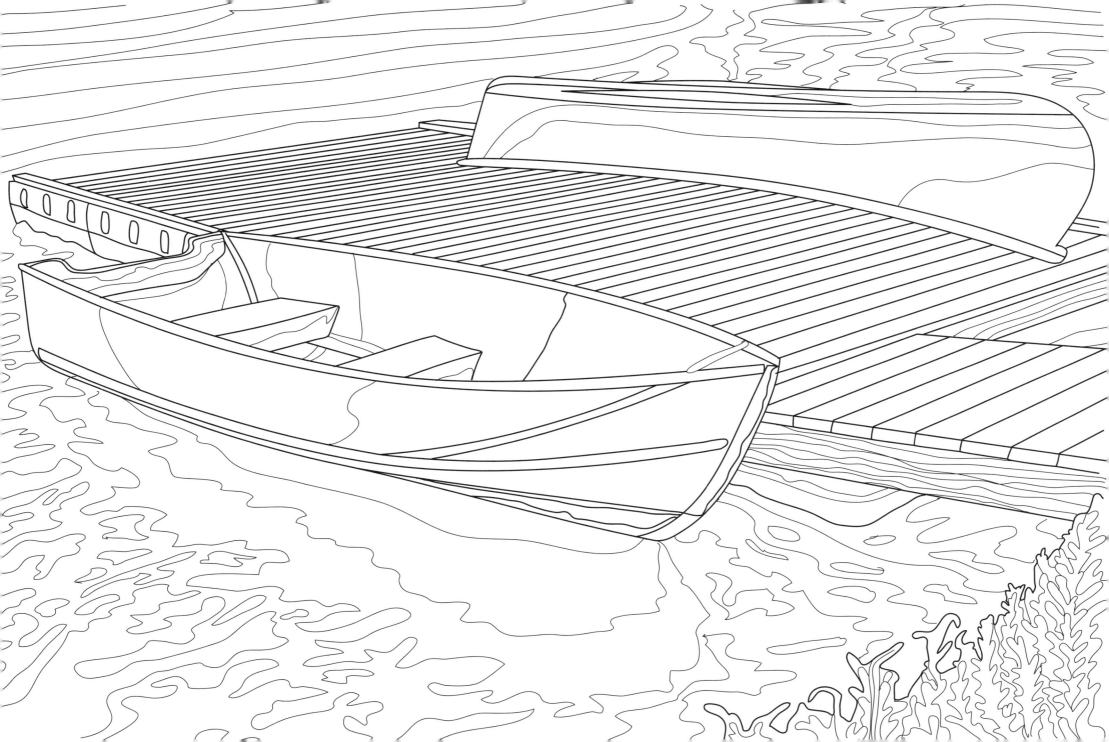

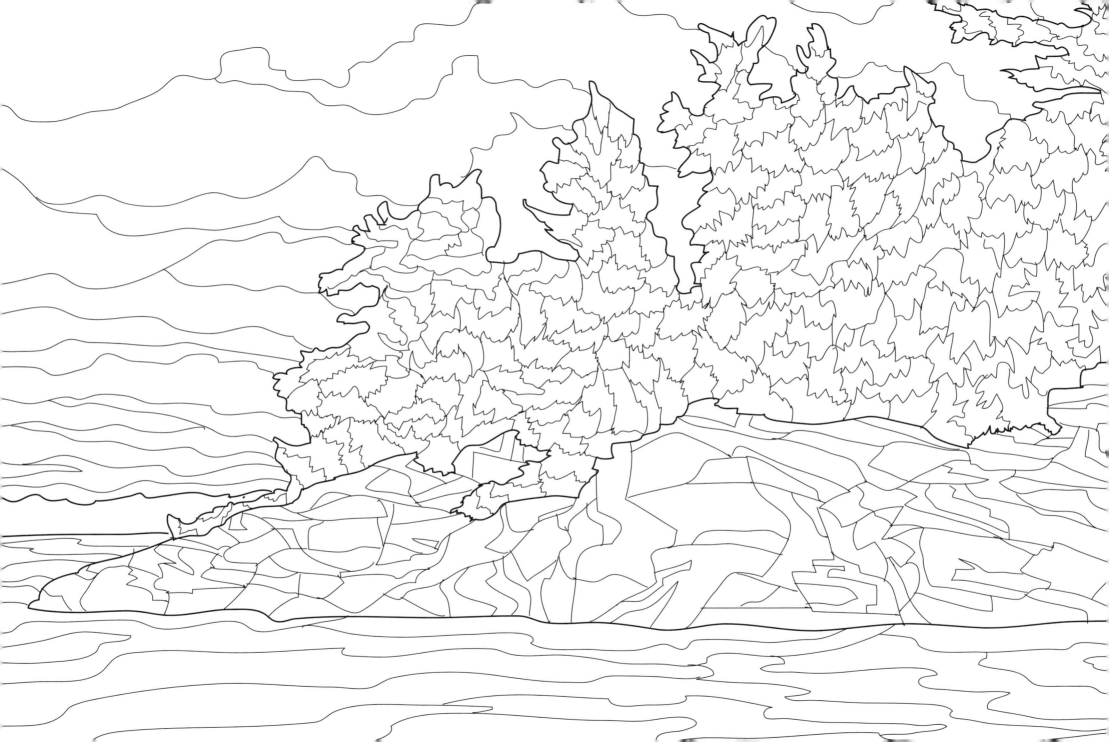

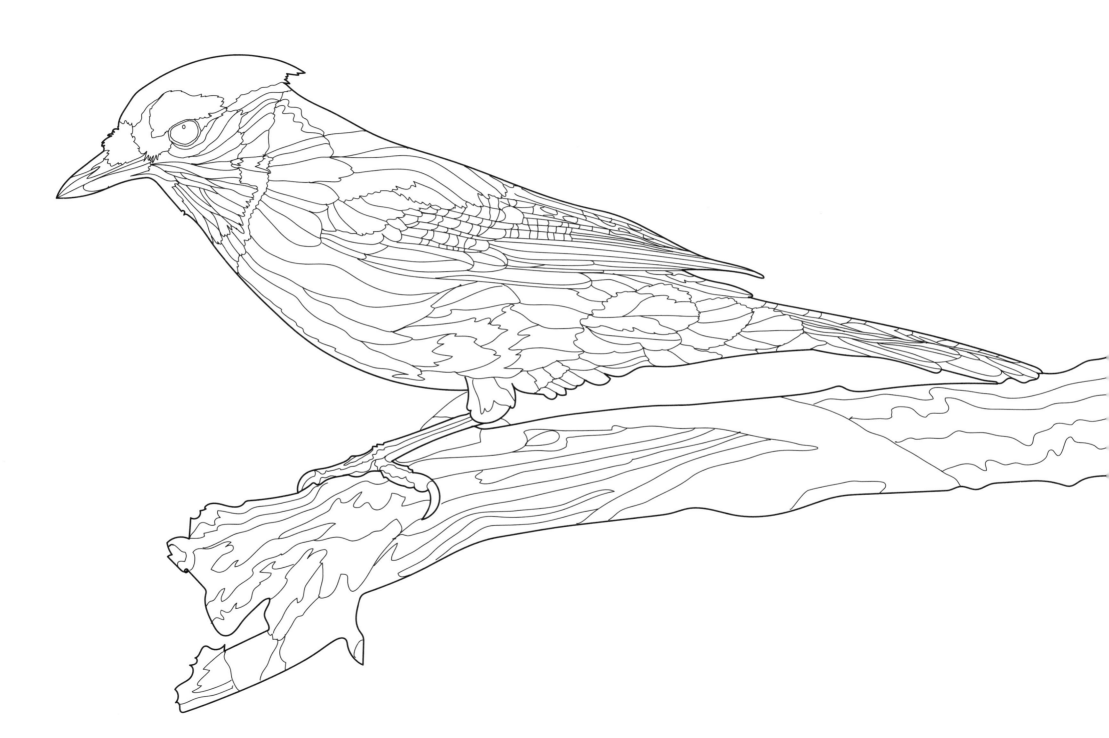

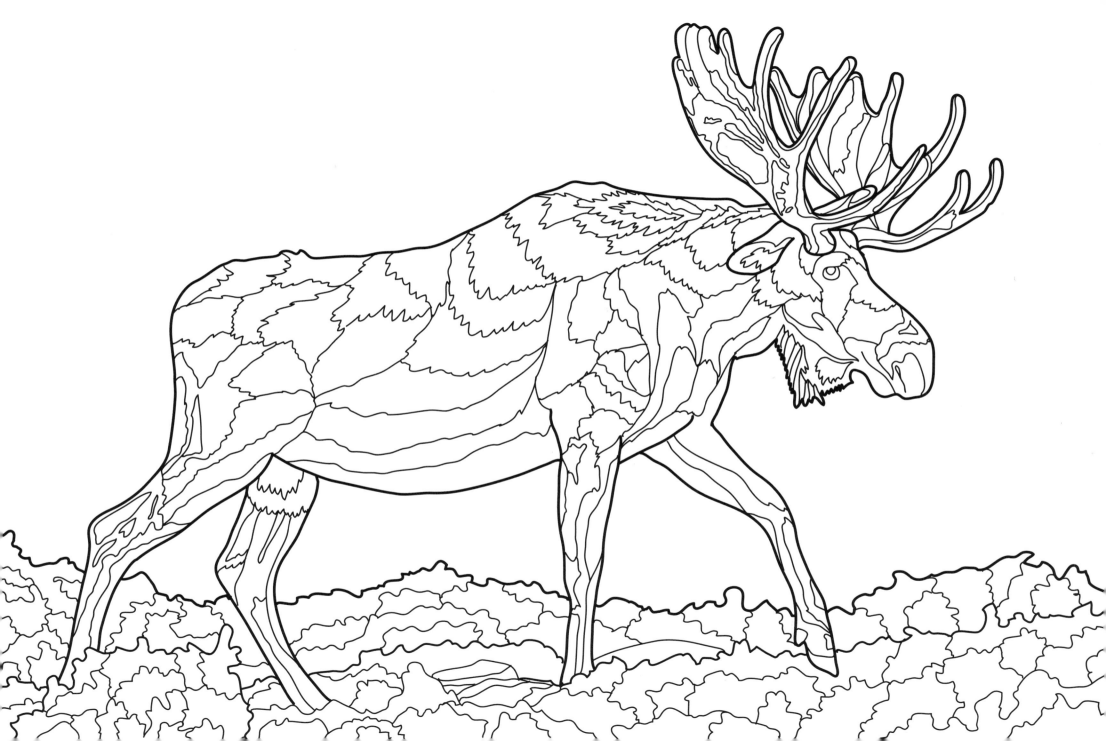

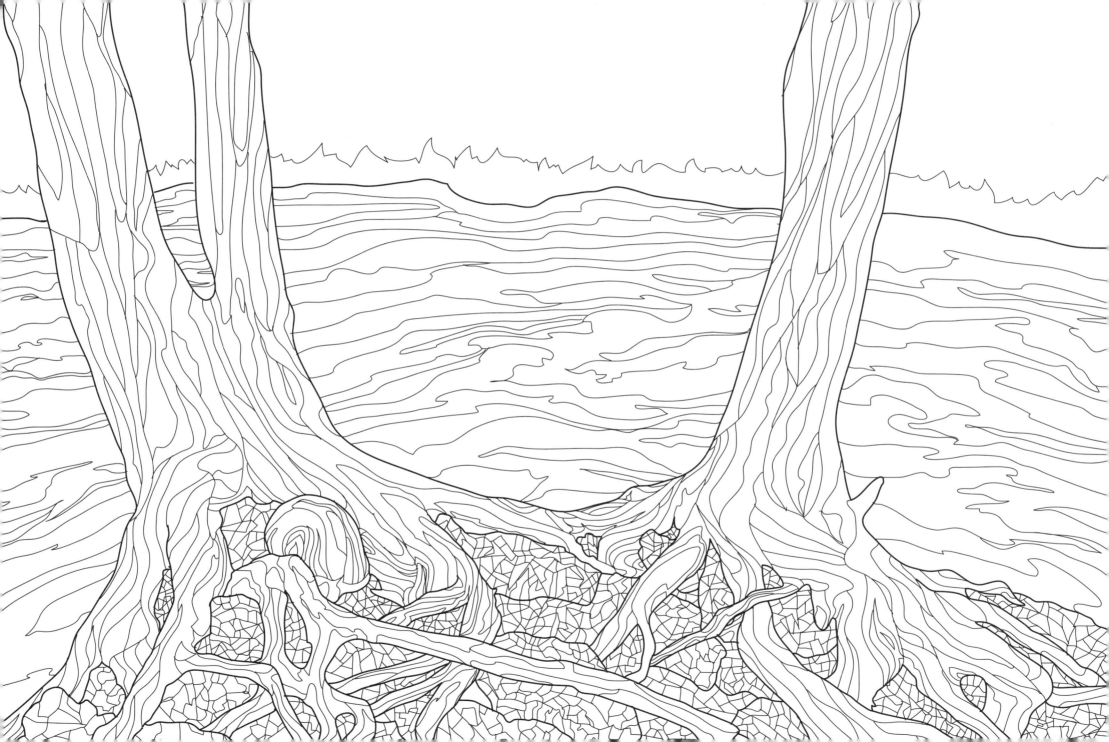

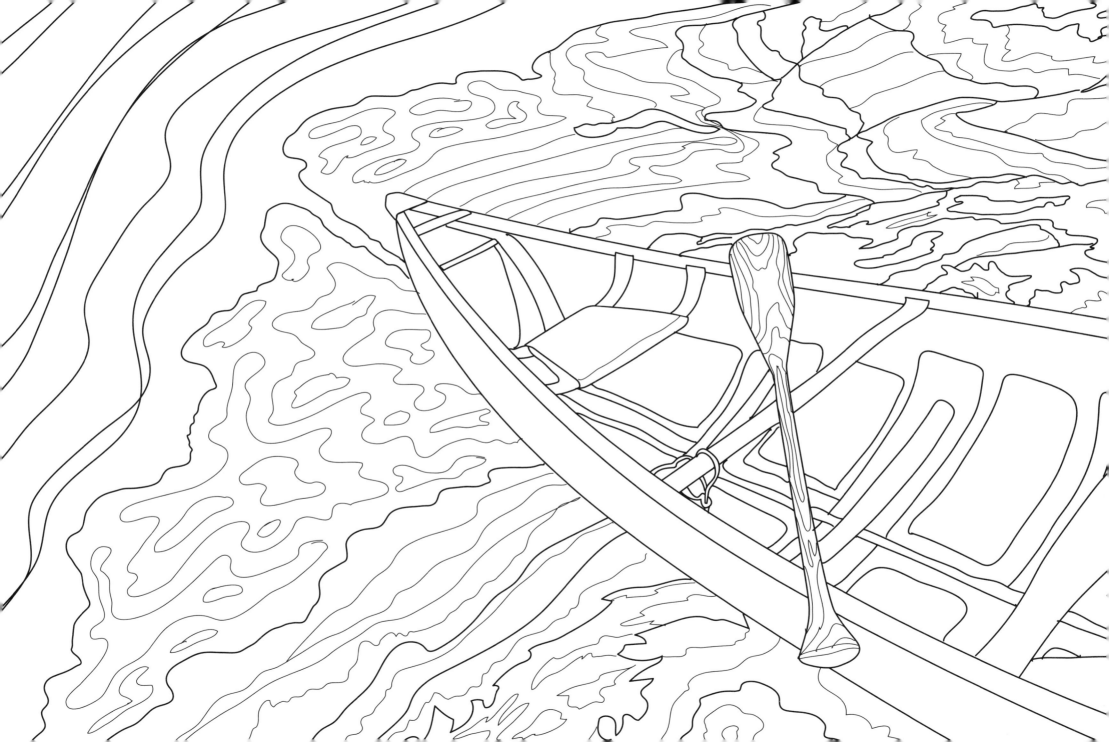

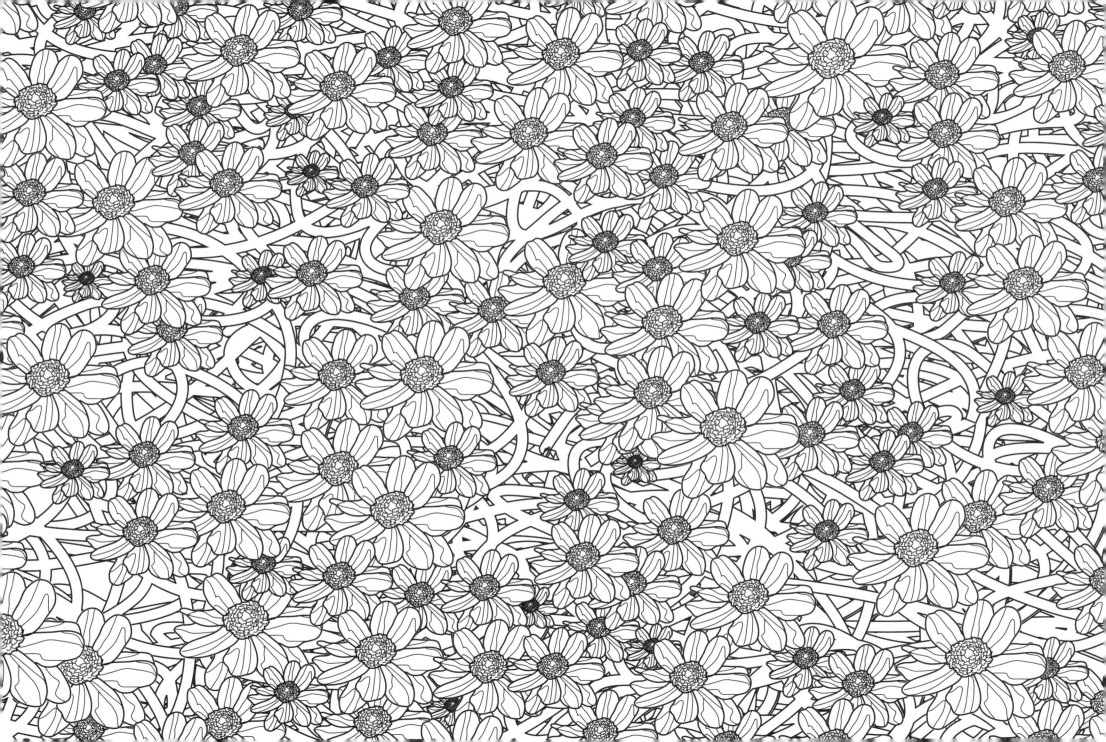

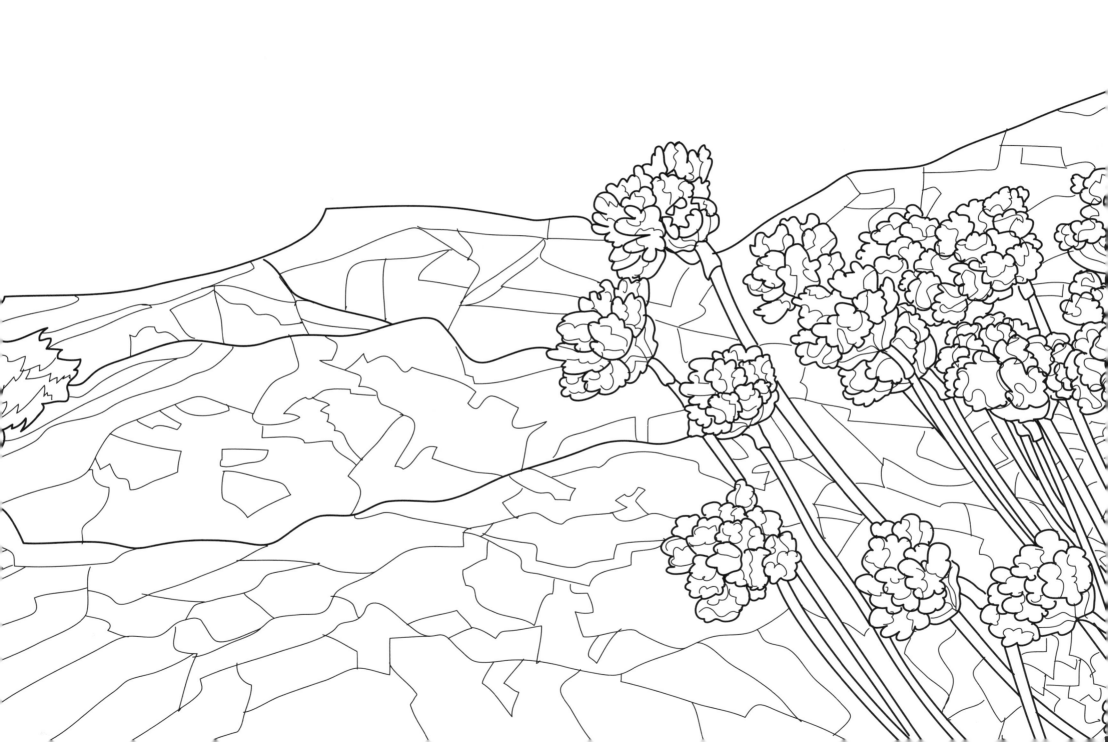

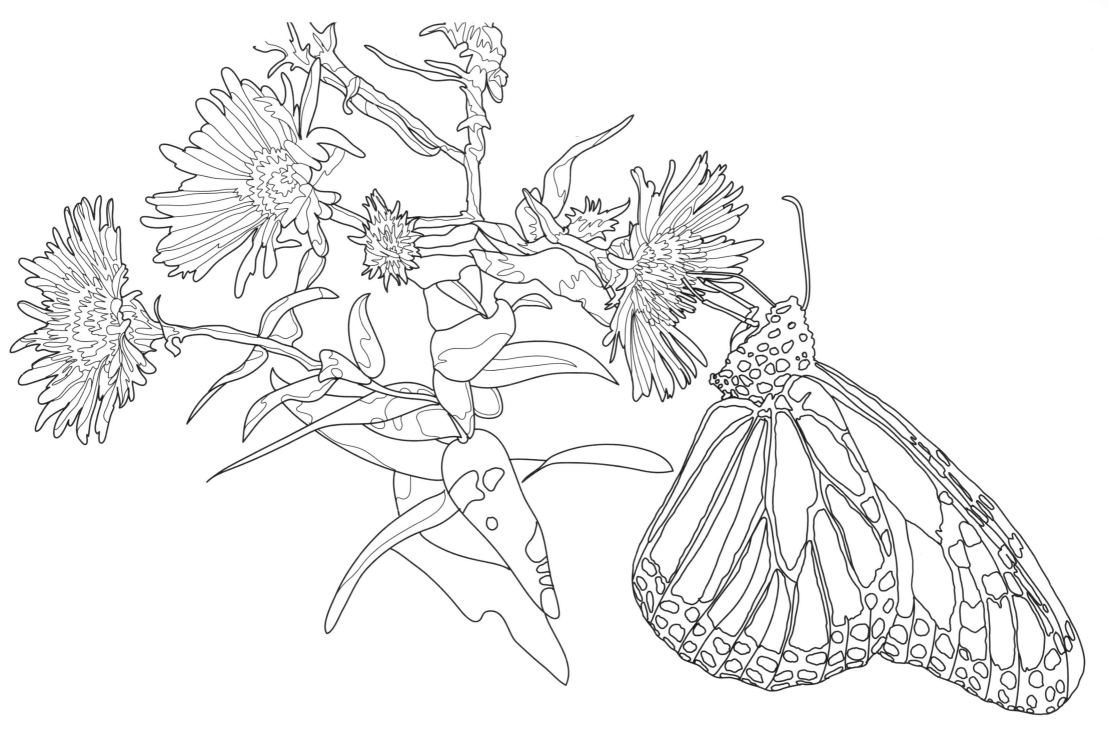

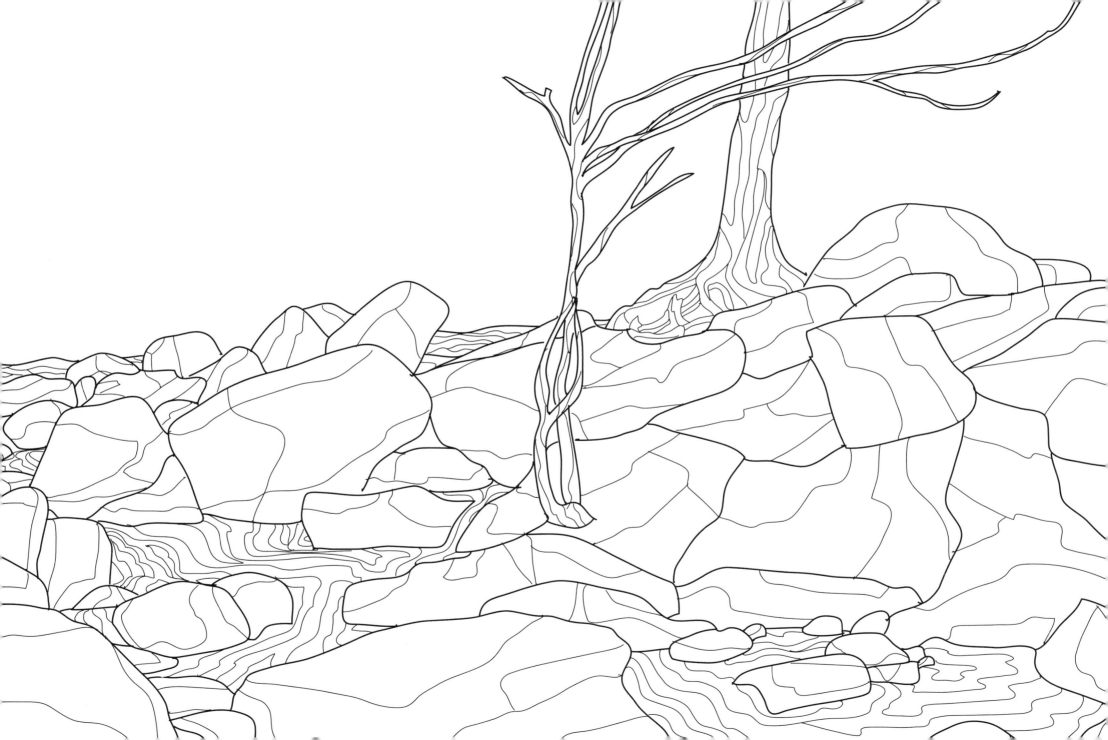

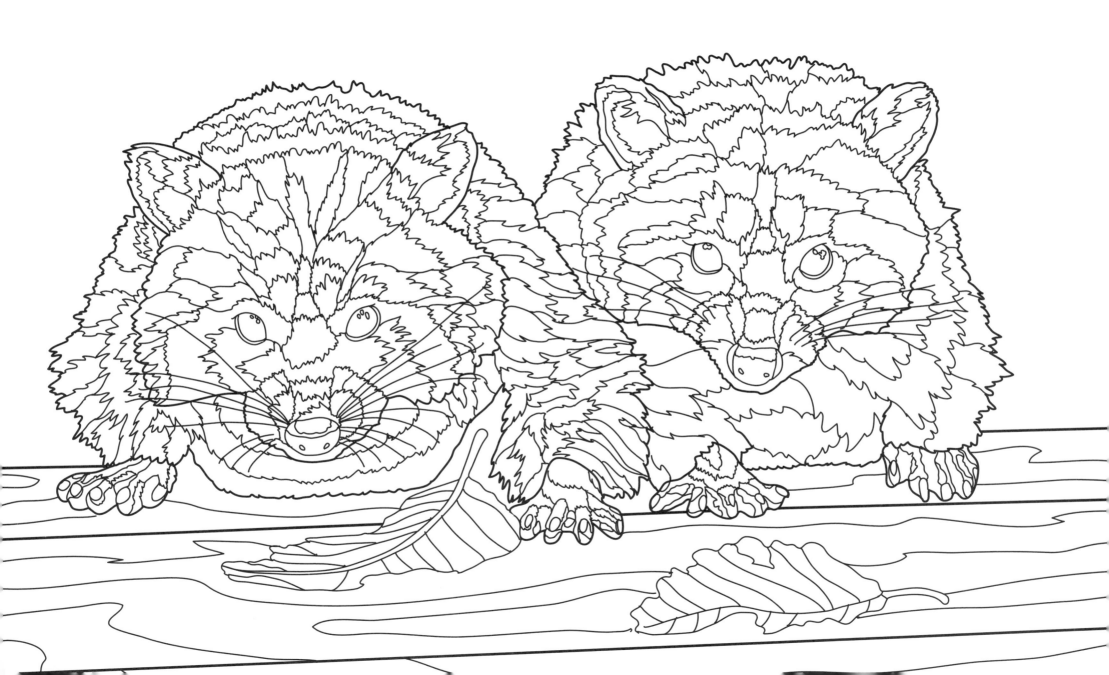

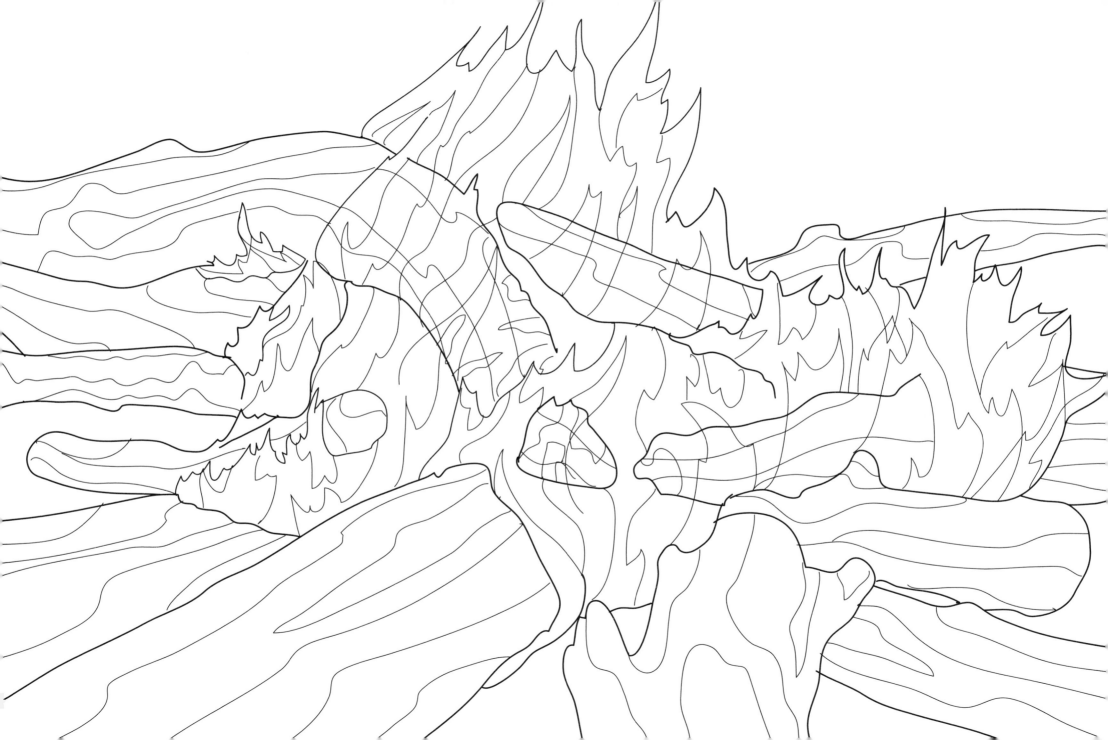

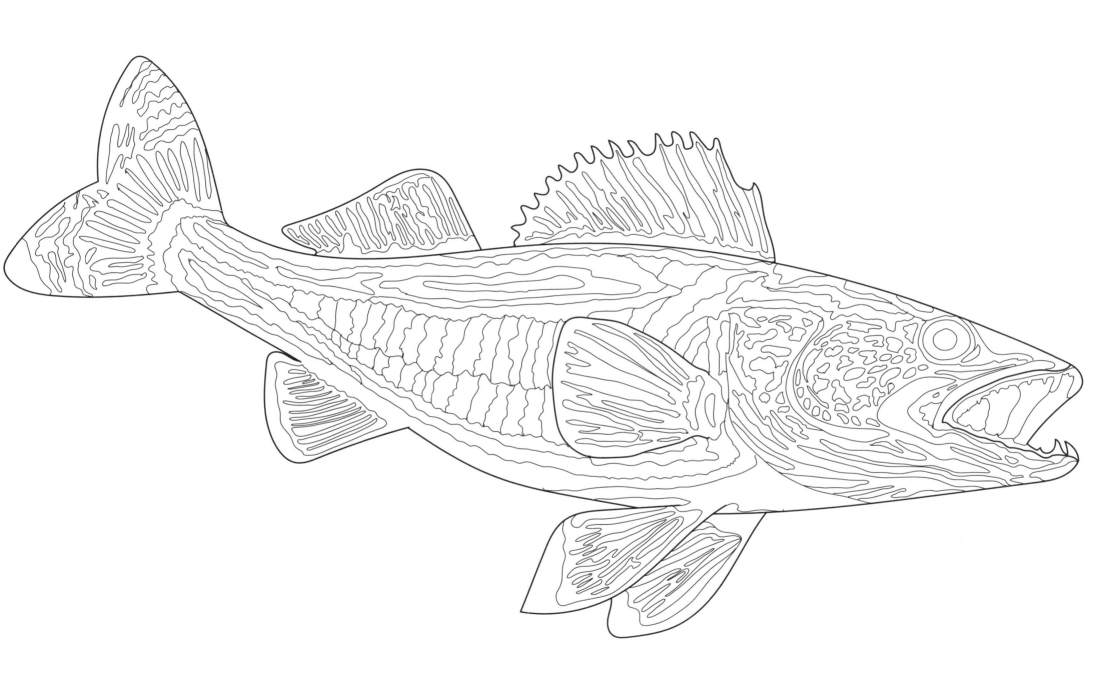

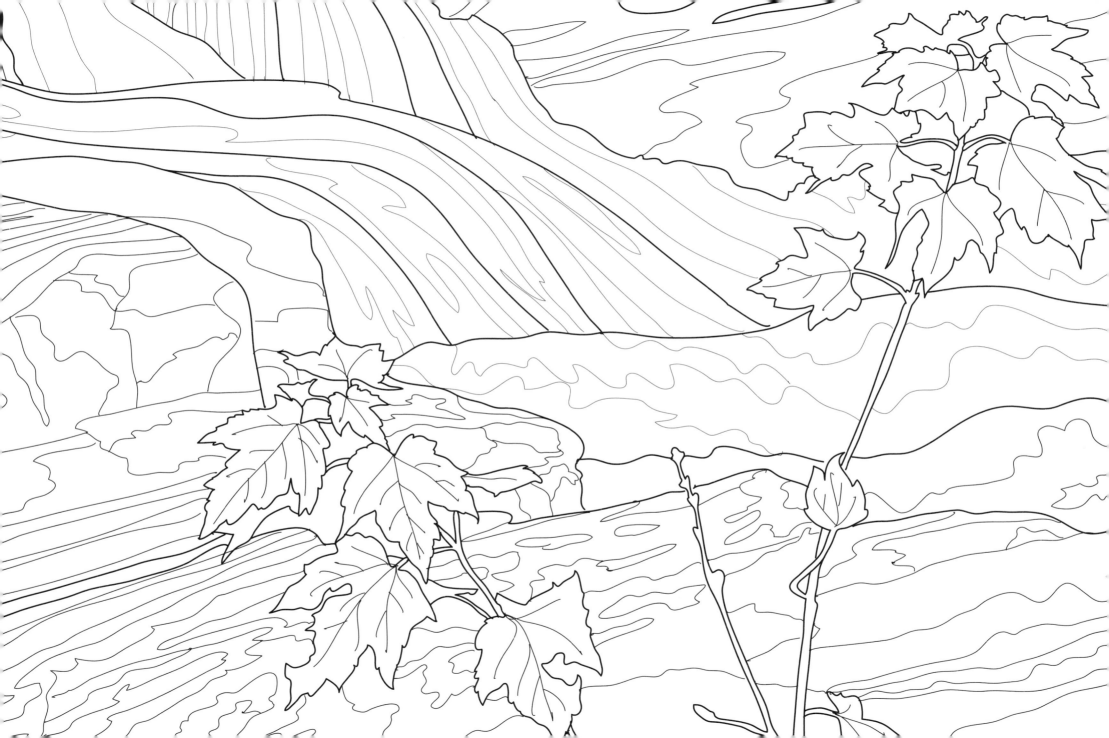

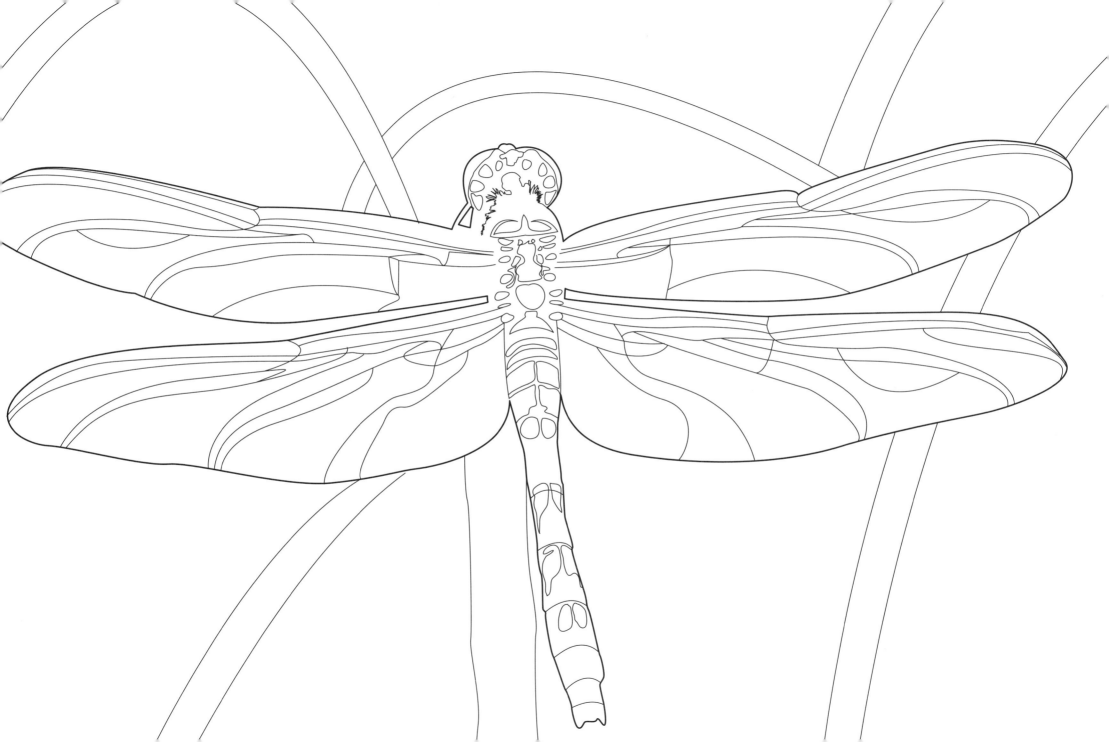

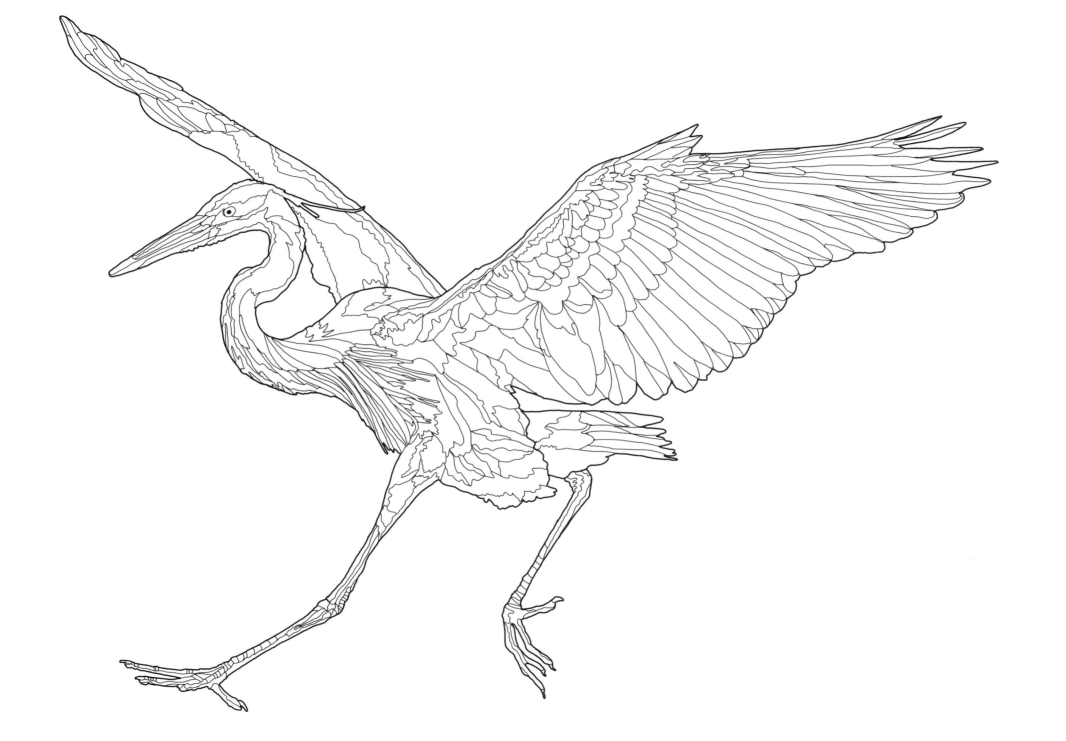

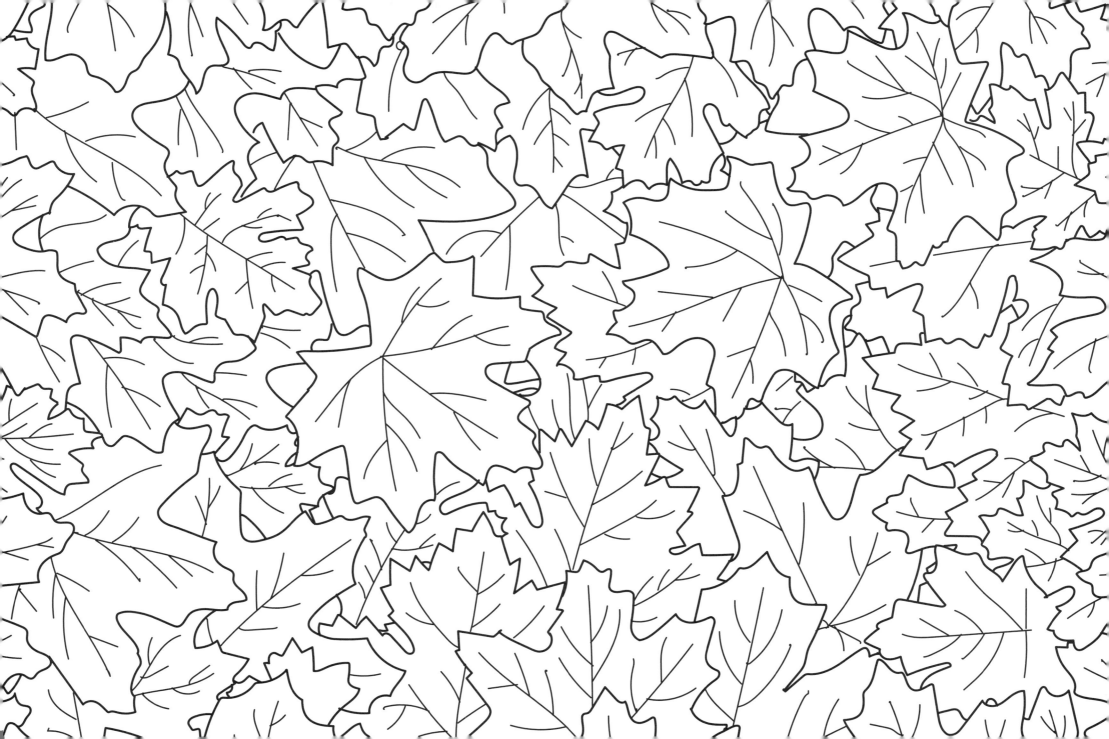

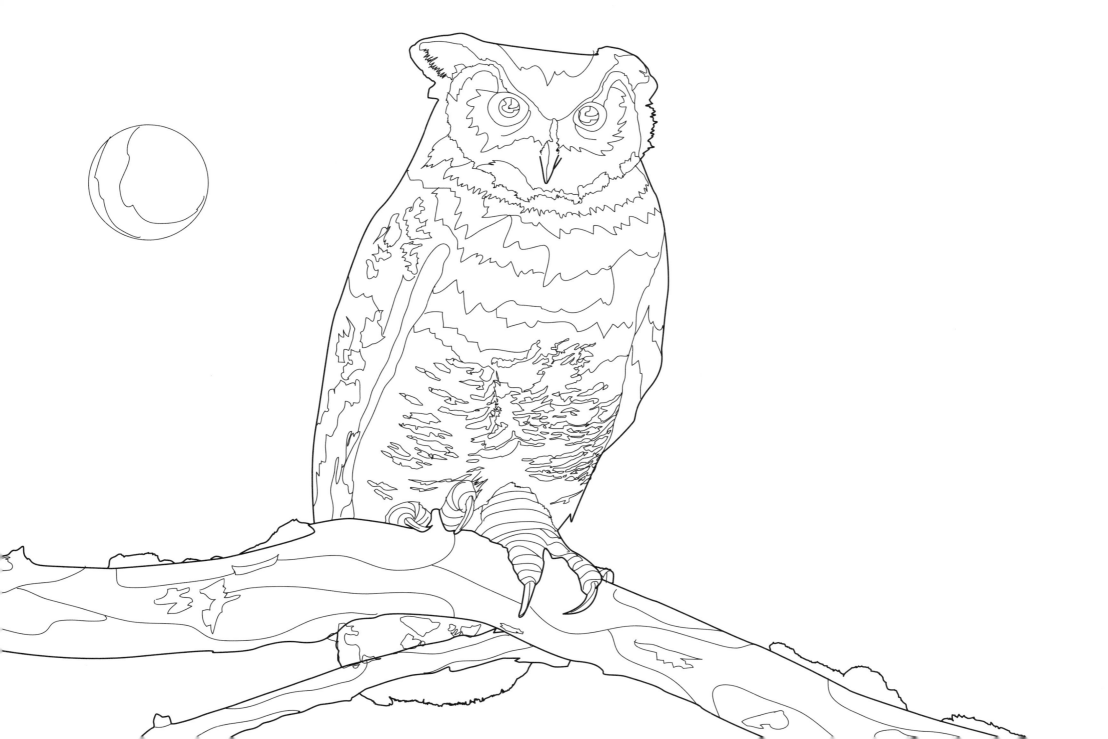

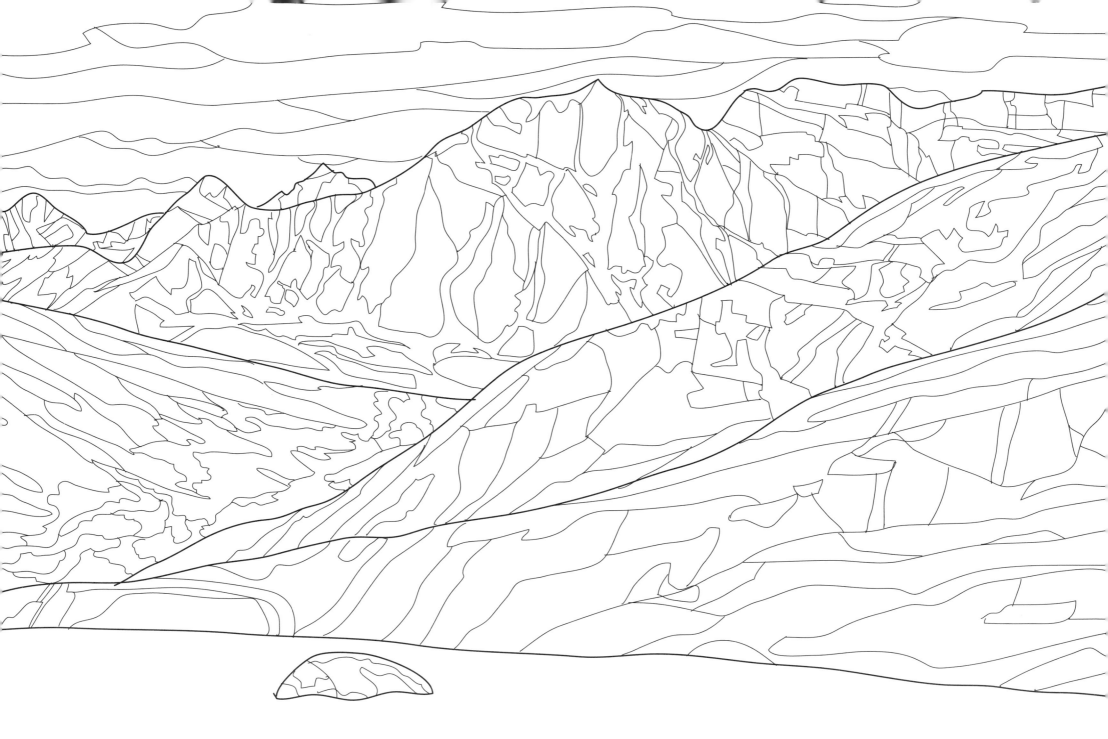

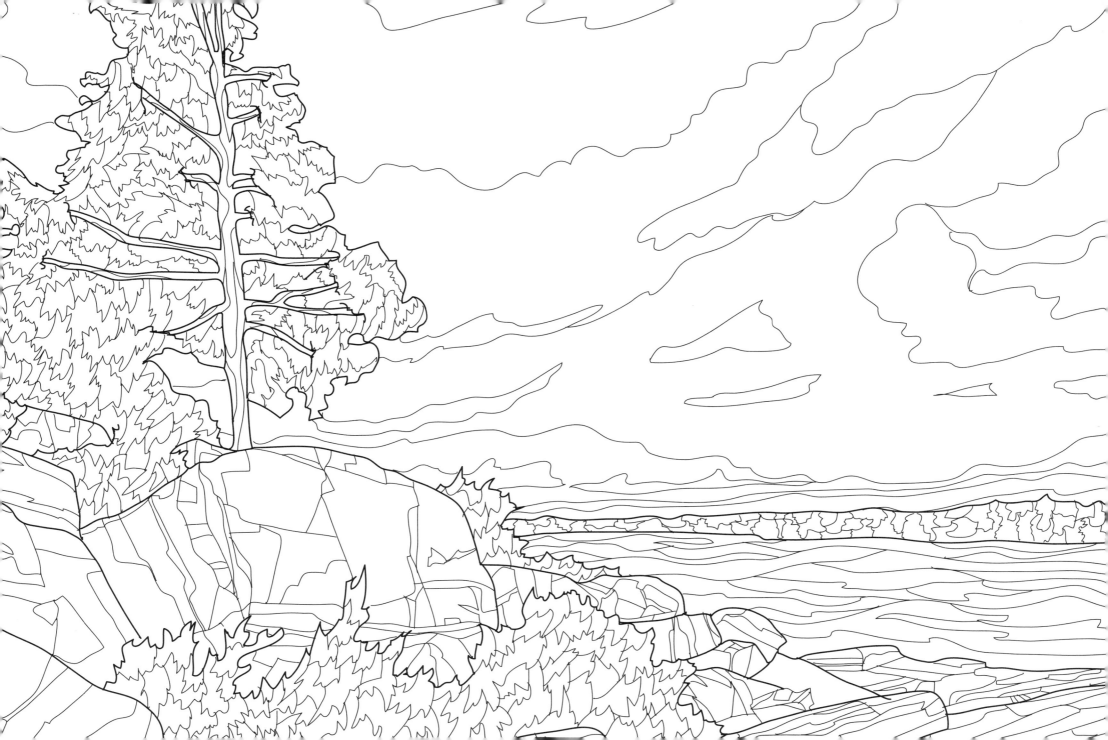

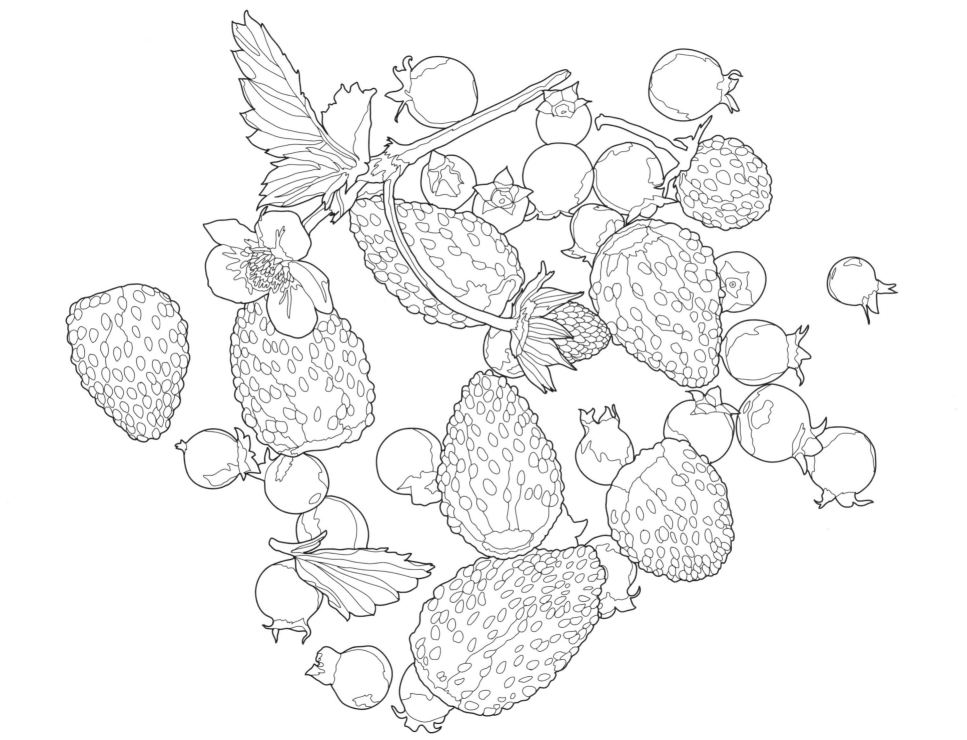

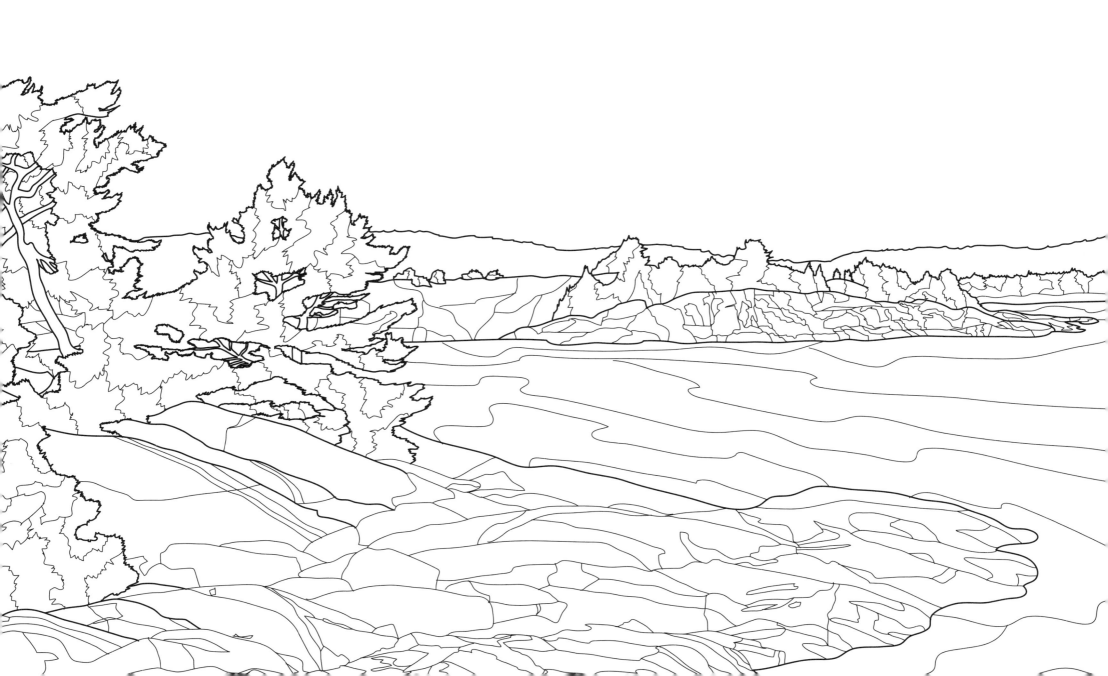

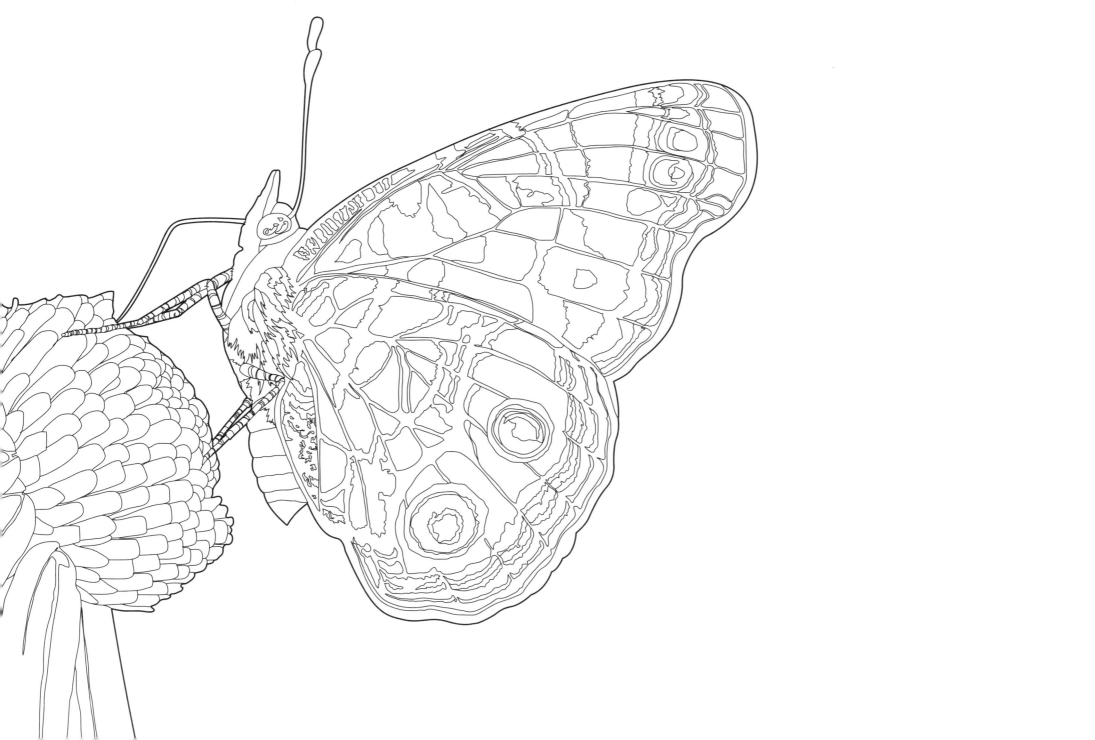

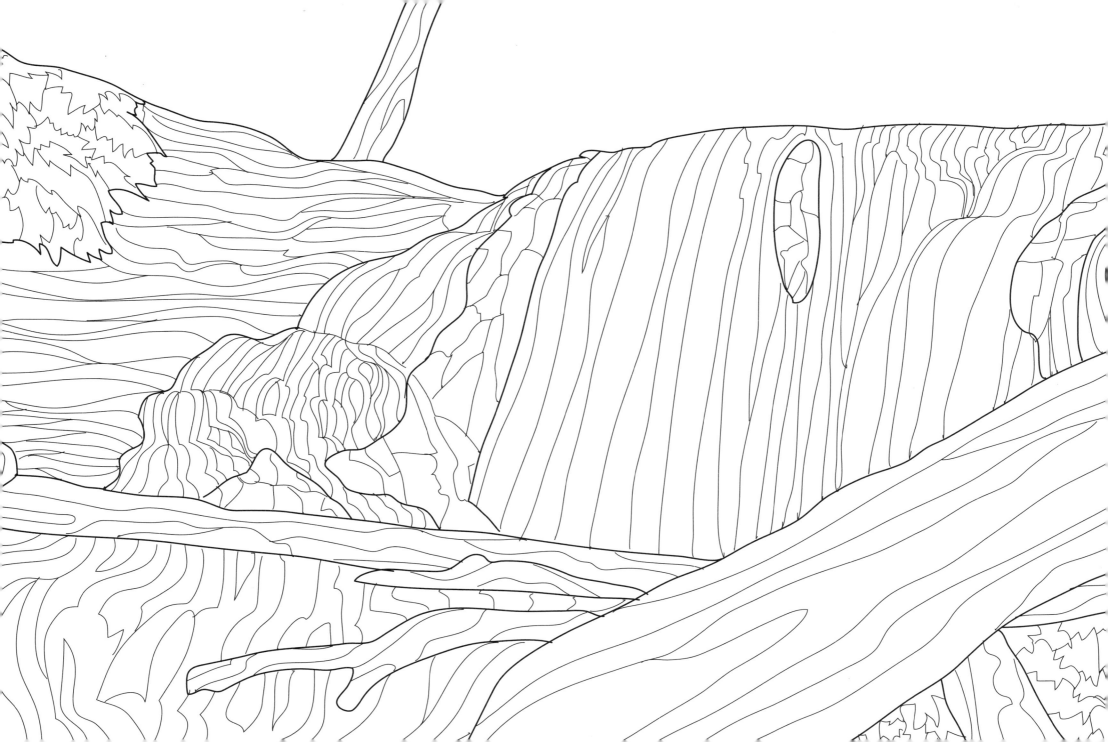

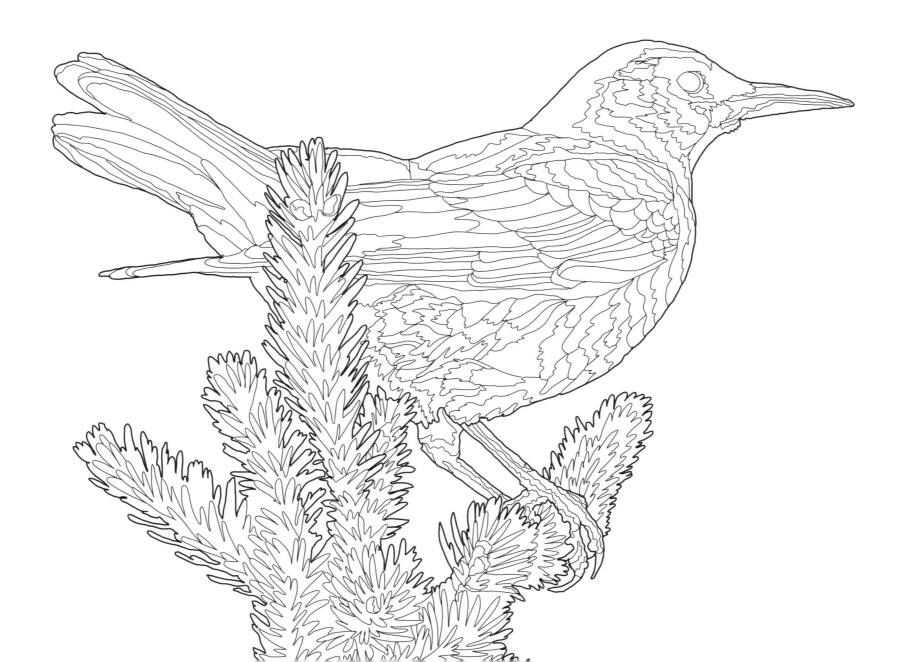

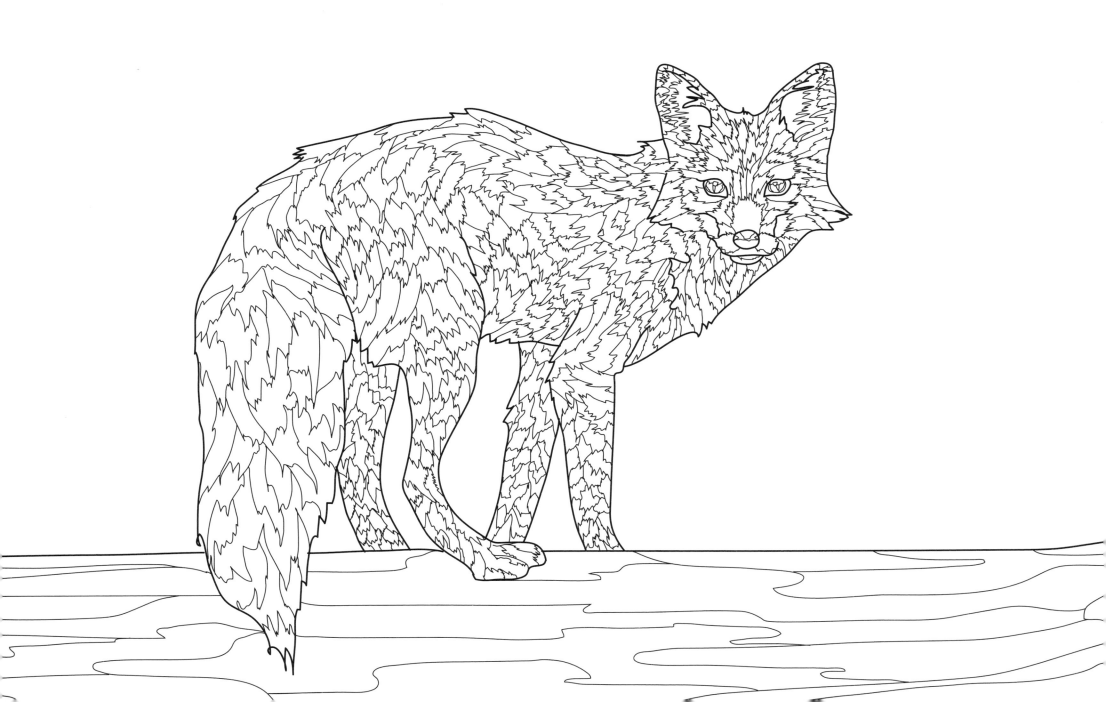

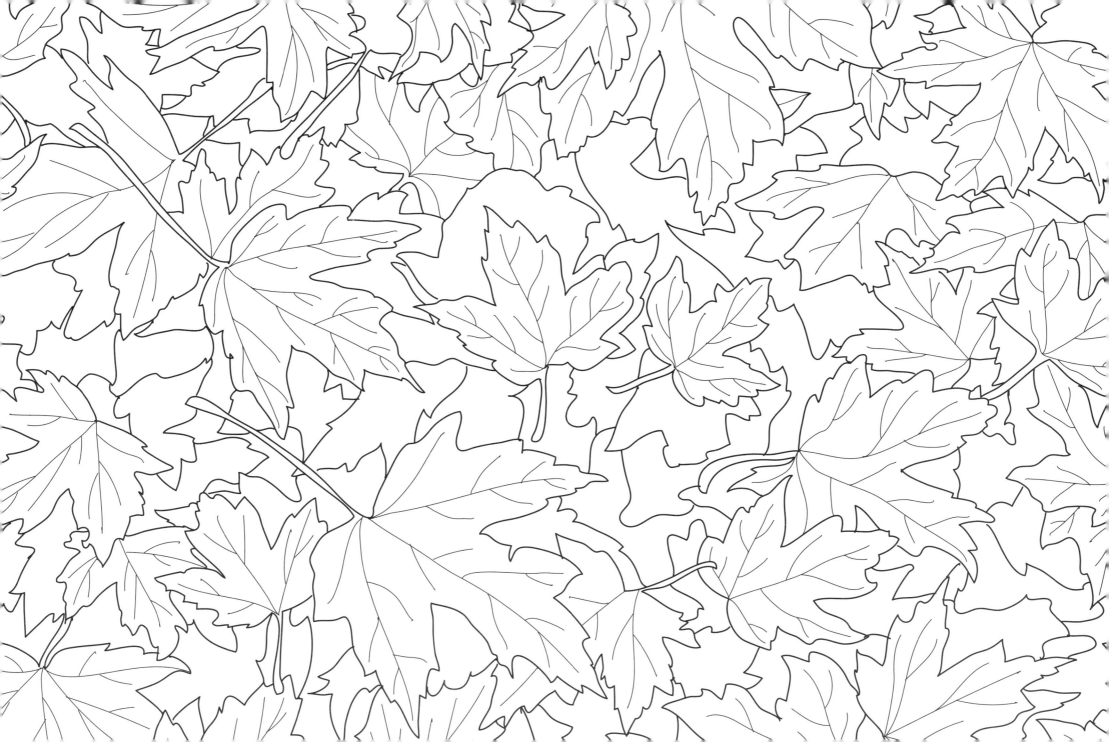